Sybil's Hut

A history & appreciation of
Farris Shepherds' Huts
of the Coombe Bissett
Steam Plough Works

by

Rollin Nicholls

First Edition 2015.

Published by Rollins Publications
Email: rollinspublications@gmail.com

A copy of this book has been deposited with the British Library.

ISBN 978-0-9931530-0-6

Book design & artwork: Julien Lightfoot, Media 4 Graphix Ltd.
Printed in England by Blackmore Press, Dorset

Dedication

*Dedicated to Sybil Spinks, granddaughter of
George Farris, of the Coombe Bissett Steam Plough
Works, for her kindness in allowing me to purchase
her own Farris hut, and generously providing and
giving permission to include some interesting and
valuable historical information and photographs
on her family's history for inclusion in my book.*

Contents

Dedication 3

Foreword (by Sybil Spinks, nee Farris) 7

Introduction 9

Sybil's Hut 10

A chance comment 11

Collecting the hut 14

History of Sybil's hut 17

The history of the Coombe Bissett
Steam Plough Works 20

Canada 24

Farris Family Tree 25

Reminiscing with Sybil 26

Farris Time line (including Sybil) 32

Coombe Bissett Steam Plough
Works Layout 34

Steam Ploughing 36

**Sybil's hut construction details
(& Farris shepherds' houses) 39**

Hut sizes 41

A typical shepherd's hut construction
(diagram) 42

Chassis 43

Body construction (granary) 45

Windows 52

Steps & doors 54

Stoves 58

Axle beams & stub axles 61

Rear axle support braces 65

Turntables 67

Front axle support bars, brake chains
& drag shoes 69

Farris wheels 72

Horse shafts 77

**Restoration of Sybil's
portable granary 82**

Inspecting the wheels 82

Inspecting the axles 83

Inspecting the chassis 86

Inspecting the body frame and
corrugated sheeting 88

A special event 89

Completing the restoration 94

Wood treatment 94

Cleaning & preserving 97

Preparation & painting the body 98

Painting the wheels 103

Attaching the granary name plate 104

George Farris name plates 107

George Farris (selection of huts) 112

John Farris name plates 118

John Farris (selection of huts) 121

Preserving huts 125

Evidence of the past 133

J Farris (& Sons). A brief overview 141

Contents

Competitors of Farris   146

Watson & Haig (of Andover)   146

Lott & Walne (of Dorchester)   147

Reeves & Sons (of Westbury)   149

Tasker & Sons (near Andover)   150

Researching other hut makers   153

Hut prices   156

Planning permission   160

Brief Construction Detailing (at a glance)   162

Collectable farming bygones   169

Types of wood   179

Model shepherds' huts   180

Steam Fairs   181

Farris shepherd's hut register   183

New discoveries (Quick References Guide)   184

Inspiration   186

Acknowledgements   192

Poems

*These poems are a selection of my favourite.
I hope you enjoy them.*

Strolling Along   8

Mindless People   19

Sounds of the night   38

Romantic Retreat   81

Lurking bodies   106

A Glimpse   124

Living with the dead   140

A space of your own   161

*The following poems, albeit not shepherd,
sheep, or hut related, are dedicated to
my best friend.*

True love   188

Floating on the breeze   189

Reflections   190

Sybil's hut

Foreword

John Farris was my great uncle. He, and his younger brother George (my grandfather) were put in charge to run the recently constructed large iron foundry workshop at Coombe Bissett in 1882. It was financed by their eldest brother, Charles, who had married an extremely wealthy lady from Berwick, St John.

They produced shepherds' houses for shepherds to live in while they tended their flocks on the downs at lambing time and at the time of the year when sheep tended to get a disease in their feet if left on wet, low lying land. The wheels were made by pouring molten metal into moulds on the floor, made from a type of tightly compressed black sand. Wheels were needed for the shepherds' houses, hen houses, and ploughs.

John soon decided to strike out on his own and founded the Shaftesbury firm making shepherds' houses, etc, which he was experienced in making with George at Coombe Bissett. The large workshop was in Haimes Lane, Shaftesbury, and their products were widely exhibited at County Shows.

John's Shaftesbury firm seems to have become a larger concern than George's in Coombe Bissett and certainly lasted longer, until the 1970's, when after the 'closing down' sale, the Bournemouth Daily Echo published a double page account of the sale.

George died in 1924 and the Coombe Bissett business continued at the Coombe Bissett foundry until 1934 with Charlie Farris, George's youngest son running it. In 1934 Charlie married and moved the business to Coombe Hill.

John died in 1914 and his sons carried on the firm until the 1970's. The name plates on both John's and George's shepherds' huts are keenly collected as are the huts themselves.

Sybil Spinks (nee Farris)
2012

Strolling along

Crunching of feet along the stony path,
The dew from branches drips to the ground,
An old timber gate leans from its rusty hinge,
Singing birds making a wonderful sound.

The view beyond is tantalisingly serene,
Softness of grasses kissing the hand,
The stroll starts to feel full of wonder,
Simplicity itself feeling ever so grand.

Eyes spot a shape on the distant horizon
Rusty and old and leaning to one side,
Brambles scrambling as if no tomorrow,
A glimmer of something trying to hide.

Remains of a lambing hut, shepherd long gone,
Body looks battered, with its door all askew,
Signs of wheels buried in the undergrowth,
Imagining how it looked when it was new.

Dreams of rescue clutter the mind,
Thoughts of abandonment never occur,
Excitement causing sentiments to ponder,
Finding the owner, forever obscure.

Weathered and beaten with the ageing of time,
Fragile but elegant in a special way,
What will become of this derelict wonder?
Time will gradually wither it away.

Sheep chomping on the grass nearby
Oblivious to the huts chequered past.
Lambs bleating in the evening twilight,
Shadows all around darkening fast.

Strolling along with the moon as a friend,
Mind still racing with increasing anticipation,
How can this beauty be eventually saved?
Emotions aroused in sweet deliberation.

Rollin

Introduction

This book is written by an enthusiast and collector of Victorian and Edwardian Farris shepherds' huts which were originally used in areas such as the South Dorset and Hampshire Downs by shepherds during the lambing season.

Based on a true story about the discovery of an original hut which he had heard about, and meeting its fascinating owner, inspired the author to write an account of the short adventure encountered, leading to its purchase and subsequent restoration.

Including historical information about George Farris and Sons of the Coombe Bissett Steam Plough Works, near Salisbury, and the excellent shepherds' huts that they produced during the late 19th century onwards, provides the reader with an authoritative and fascinating insight of this company in bygone days.

Useful construction details, information, and advice on the sympathetic approach required during the restoration of these remarkable portable huts, emphasises the importance towards the preservation of a small piece of our rural history.

Also included are details of George's brother, John Farris of Shaftesbury, and a few other local competitors.

Rollin Nicholls

Rollin Nicholls & his restored hut.

Sybil's Hut

Shepherds' huts, also known as shepherds' houses, were extensively used by downland shepherds during the 19th and early 20th centuries, providing temporary shelter and sleeping accommodation whilst lambing was in progress. Sick and orphaned lambs could also be housed in a hut for a day or two, to offer warmth during the early hours of their lives. They were also a useful storage facility for tools, medicines, and general equipment.

Conditions were harsh and very basic for shepherds, but a hut, although a little draughty, did give some protection from the elements. A table, stool and bed was usually included, and a tiny stove could provide heating and cooking facilities, enabling the shepherd to warm milk in a saucepan for young lambs, or boil water for his own use. Firewood or coal could be used on the stove. There was no toilet, or bath, and storage space was very limited.

Shepherds were highly respected by their employer, as sheep were regarded as a valuable commodity during the 19th century, with the wool industry being at its most affluent. They would have been provided with a hut during the lambing season as well as offered a home on the farm.

Lighting was traditionally from a tin candle lantern, with windows made of horn, and preferred by shepherds as they were safer to use than later tin lanterns with glass. Such lanterns could confidently be used in the hut as well as amongst the sheep folds during lambing. Folds were constructed from hurdles and were also used to confine sheep to specific areas, such as when winter feeding them on turnips, or when being sold at market.

 Early portable shepherds' huts were originally made of wood, but during the late 19th century, companies such as Farris made sturdy examples consisting of a strong wooden chassis on substantial cast iron wheels, with galvanised corrugated sheeting on the outside, and wooden panelling on the inside.

A chance comment

As an enthusiast and collector of original shepherds' huts and related items, I was keen to investigate a comment from a friend who knew someone who had been to see a shepherd's hut at Coombe Bissett, near Salisbury, reputedly to be in poor condition, and thought it might be for  sale. The comment from my friend was along the lines 'what might be rough to him may not be too bad to you or me'. My curiosity was growing.

I had previously heard about this hut earlier in the year whilst visiting The Great Dorset Steam Fair (2011), but all reports indicated that it was a bit of a wreck. However, such images of these unique living spaces constantly turn over in my mind, and I felt it was worth having a day off work to go and look for myself, and who knows, some of the parts, such as the wheels, or remains of an original stove, may come in useful for another project.

So, on the 4th December 2011, I set off on a three hour drive to Coombe Bissett, with the company of my dog, Pepper, not really knowing if I would find the hut or its owner. Armed with a map and some emergency rations (e.g. food and drink) my adventure had begun. I could feel my adrenalin racing!

I had kindly been given some rough directions of its location by my friend, and was told to drive out of Salisbury on the A 354, and as I came into Coombe Bissett, it was standing on the bank where the original Farris Works used to be situated. 'You can't miss it!'

Well, I didn't miss it, thank goodness. There it was, all by itself, situated at the top of a bank.

There were two Victorian red bricked semi detached cottages adjacent to the field where the hut was standing, so I knocked loudly on the front door of the one on the right. No answer, so I knocked louder. Still no answer!

I strolled around the back of this cottage and knocked on the back door. Still no one answered.

Old Foundry cottages.

With a little trepidation, I then proceeded to go to the second cottage, situated on the left side, and all I could see there were two huge dogs looking at me. I'm good with dogs but my common sense told me not to be too persistent, so I decided to return to my vehicle to rethink my plan.

On the way back to my vehicle, the owner of the second cottage returned home, and after a brief conversation with this helpful neighbour, I was told to go around the back of the first cottage and knock very loudly, as the owner of the hut was an elderly lady who was a little hard of hearing.

I knocked very loudly on the back door, calling out, so as not to frighten the elderly lady, especially as I was a man whom she didn't know. The door opened, and I politely introduced myself.

I said I was a shepherd's hut enthusiast, and presented her with an introductory letter with my personal details on, and a brief description that I would be interested in purchasing her hut. I was actually intending to leave this letter in it if I couldn't find the owner, but it seemed appropriate to give it to this lady now.

They always say the first few seconds of an introduction are the most important, and I think she could see I was fairly knowledgeable about shepherds' houses, and I let my enthusiasm do the rest. She was certainly surprised, and possibly impressed, that I had made the effort to drive about three hours to Coombe Bissett, which could so easily have resulted in disappointment.

This charming, elderly lady, was Sybil, the granddaughter of George Farris who originally made the hut which I had come to see, and we were soon having an interesting chat about her grandfathers business that used to be located there.

Sybil was quite a petite lady, and although she used a stick, she was remarkably agile for her age. She was certainly very knowledgeable about her family history, being particularly quick on dates, and was happy to show me an article she had previously written, including family photographs. I felt very welcome, and it was obvious we had similar interests regarding her family and their shepherds' houses.

I was then asked what I would be prepared to pay, so as not to insult her with a ridiculously low offer, I offered my maximum figure, but added that I would prefer to deal with one of her sons, or daughters, if it was acceptable, remembering how it used to annoy me when people used to take advantage of my own mother in her later years. Sybil was not slow to inform me that she had a daughter and that they had been offered this amount previously.

This is the point where one thinks their reasonable offer and negotiating skills are taking a tumble, so I asked if I could go and have a closer look at her hut. Sybil said this was not a problem as long as I did not go inside, as there was a man who occasionally lived in it and stored some of his possessions there. She also added that someone had recently attempted to steal it by cutting through the fence, near the road, and tried to tow it away, but were unable to as the wheels were seized. She could obviously see how shocked I was about this news!

On closer inspection, I could see it looked in remarkably good overall condition for its age, and was painted green on the side panels, with black roof and red wheels. To an enthusiast, it looked very beautiful, perhaps a little 'weathered' around the edges, but this was to be expected.

Peering underneath, the chassis and floor appeared to look reasonably sound, whilst the wooden axles had signs of the normal age related wear on the ends. The corrugation was in overall very good condition, with only the ends of the roof panels, and the rear panel adjacent to the door, needing additional attention and repair. I was certainly impressed with the condition of the wheels, as some Farris wheels can be found in quite poor condition.

A sneaky look through the top door showed that there was no internal wooden panelling present, and that someone had taken up residence in it. There was a bed and associated paraphernalia that one would expect if someone was living there.

I noticed that the bolts that attach the stub axles to the rear axle beam had sheared off, resulting in the seized rear wheels tipping inwards against the body. Apart from this, there appeared to be no serious damage.

Quickly returning back to Sybil's cottage, I was unable to control my excitement, and told her it was lovely, and immediately increased my offer. She appeared pleased and then presented me with her daughter's name, address and telephone number and advised me to 'phone her after six' that evening.

I thanked Sybil for her time and the conversation about her family history, and then briskly drove home in order to phone her daughter later on.

Apprehensively, I phoned Sybil's daughter, Angela, and found her to be as charming and helpful as her mother. It must have been my lucky day as we agreed on a reasonable price for the hut, and Angela said that although many other people wanted to buy it (she appeared to have a long list of names and telephone numbers of interested people) her mother wanted me to have it. I felt very privileged!

Collecting the hut

On 12th December 2011, I found myself back down at Coombe Bissett collecting my latest purchase. Sybil and Angela had very kindly and generously sorted out some interesting family photographs and history, including some on the Steam Plough Works at Coombe Bissett. Sybil commented that 'she had hardly slept for a week as she was worried someone would return and steal the hut and wheels'. I know the feeling!

Sybil had invited me into her cottage and was keen to chat about her grandfather, family and the Steam Plough Works. It was quite surreal to be sitting in the family front living room, where George Farris used to relax with his family, in front of an open fire, and finding myself chatting to his granddaughter and looking at old family photographs.

The front living room was not huge, but seemed very cosy with its slate fire surround as a centre piece. The furniture was of the same period as the cottage, making the room appear timeless, as if George Farris had just left it to be enjoyed by future generations.

Sybil was on very good form and was especially helpful with answering any questions that I had about her ancestors. I must admit, I was desperately trying to jot down notes during our conversation without appearing rude, as I didn't want to forget any of the details that she was giving to me. I was finding our conversation incredibly interesting, and to be listening to Sybil reminiscing about her grandfather was fascinating and informative.

Jim, the last occupant of Sybil's hut at Coombe Bissett.

Waiting outside, the 'hut resident' called Jim (in his 50's) was also in attendance and was watching the collection of it with much interest. Jim appeared quite an eccentric person, and actually had a slight resemblance to an old shepherd with long beard and dressed for the unpredictable English weather, in gaiters, boots and waterproofs. I was feeling a little guilty as his things had been removed from the hut by Angela a few days previously and stored in a shed nearby, and his temporary dwelling was soon to be removed, which must have left him with some mixed emotions, especially as events were happening so quickly. His alternative accommodation was a tent that he pitched on the edge of the original foundry site, just to the rear of Sybil's cottage.

Angela referred to Jim as 'kind, gentle, educated, very well spoken, good humoured, with lots of natural wisdom and plenty of time to reflect, and is one more piece of history of the shepherd's hut'.

Sybil was very happy to have some photographs taken of her, inside and outside of her hut, and kindly climbed up the steps and signed her maiden name 'Sybil Farris 2011' on the inside of the corrugated sheeting. For a lady in her 94th year (aged 95 the following April) she was truly amazing, and her name will live on in this hut indefinitely.

Eddie Butterfield, a shepherd's hut expert from Bere Regis was also on hand helping to organise the professional and very careful recovery of my new project from the site. It is crucial to ensure that considerate and experienced help is available in order to avoid any unnecessary damage. The rear wheels needed to be straightened and strapped, and then it was slowly skidded along the field before being carefully craned over the fence onto a flat bed lorry. This was felt to be the best option as the ground was wet and soft and we couldn't risk the lorry becoming stuck.

Sybil's signature

Sybil & her hut.

Luckily, the ponies in the field were behaving themselves, which made the recovery procedure easier. Sybil had provided some food for them in case they became a nuisance and tried to escape. It would have been a nightmare if they had found a way out and had made their way briskly down the A 354 with us in pursuit.

The hut was gradually lifted onto the lorry (which incorporated a heavy duty crane) and appeared huge as it was lowered and positioned into place. Straps were used around the axles and wheels to secure it. The height of it positioned on the lorry was very useful for checking the chassis, axles, and under the floorboards. I could feel my heart racing with excitement!

Sybil had returned to her cottage as she was becoming tired, so I went and said thank you and goodbye before leaving. It must have been an exhausting day for her, with a mixture of sadness

Loaded and ready to transport to its restorers.

and mixed emotions, but also relief as her hut had found a good home.

Once everything was ready, the lorry was gradually reversed back onto the main road and then drove down to Bere Regis where an overall assessment of my new purchase could be carried out more accurately, and the stub axles could be removed. The wheels were to be soaked in diesel and if necessary put into a press to free them from the stub axles and it was certainly a job for an expert who had previous experience in this operation.

On closer inspection and assessment of the original front axle, it was thought that it would probably need replacing with an exact copy, as the ends were quite fragile and would cause problems, especially when removing the worn axle securing bolts.

The rear axle, hopefully, would only need some glue and bracing in order to make it serviceable again. There were also signs of a bit of deterioration on the rear chassis member where the rear step brackets were located. This work could be carried out whilst the seized wheels were being freed, and once completed, the hut could then be transported to my home for further restoration and preservation.

History of Sybil's hut

Sybil's hut was bought for Sybil by her daughter, Angela (great granddaughter of George Farris) in 2002, as she thought it would be lovely to display an original example back at the Coombe Bissett foundry. It was discovered by her on an isolated farmyard in Box, Wiltshire, and was previously owned by a farmer called Frederick Gaulstone. His father had bought it from a machinery sale in Devizes in the 1940's, and towed it back to Box with his tractor. It was used as a general purpose store for many years, including keeping chicken corn in it.

Sybil's hut discovered at Box, Wiltshire. Photo Sybil Spinks.

Six decades later, Angela had made her discovery whilst out walking with a rambling group, and says 'it was in a terrible state'. It had been resting amongst a pile of old tyres behind a derelict chicken shed. The name plate confirmed it was a genuine G. Farris hut, so she persuaded the farmer to sell it to her, and had it transported back to the Coombe Bissett site where it had originally been built approximately 100 years before. There appears to have been quite a gathering of family members to welcome it home after all those years!

Displaying it back at the original site was a wonderful reminder to the type of work carried out at the foundry and a tribute to the family and hard workers who lived and laboured there.

Sybil reminisced whilst sitting in her grandfathers old cottage and said she 'remembers a shepherd's hut always standing at the top of the bank in front of the Coombe Bissett Steam Plough Works to advertise the agricultural foundry'.

She also stated that 'unfortunately, all that remains of the original Works is the old two way water pump. The rest of the building was blown down in the 1960's gale as it was only made of corrugated iron'.

It's incredible how corrugated iron has actually been a blessing in disguise for the Shepherd's hut design, as it has provided a sturdy weatherproof covering which has increased the durability of them. As an enthusiast, I now look at a piece of corrugated iron with a completely different perspective than I used to.

Sybil's hut at the Coombe Bissett foundry. The original foundry water pump is in the foreground. Photo Sybil Spinks.

In the years that followed, Sybil's hut soon became a local landmark and had many admirers, and the family had a considerable amount of offers made to buy it. The attempted theft, which was a huge worry for Sybil, and the possibility of Sybil eventually moving to a new home, were two of the main influences regarding the sale of it to me. Angela says 'I took her Mum's fancy' which referred to Sybil liking me as she knew her hut was going to an enthusiast and a good home, and I could be trusted to preserve it for future generations to enjoy.

It appears some local residents of Coombe Bissett were 'bitterly disappointed' it had been sold, and some had expressed their wishes to buy it. I had obviously been lucky and had been in the right place at the right time. Everyone would have been disappointed if it had been stolen and broken up and sold for scrap. In a way, it was rescued by an enthusiast before it was taken and that has to be a good outcome.

My poem 'Mindless People' was influenced by the attempted theft of Sybil's hut. I have felt very honoured that Sybil chose me to look after her hut, as it had been a present from her daughter to display on the original Farris premises. I also feel privileged with the kindness and generosity of information that she has offered to me and that we have got on so well.

Mindless people

Wire cutters defacing mesh,
Arrogance defies common sense,
Their aim is to steal without remorse,
No matter what the consequence.

Slowly figures appear in the night,
Hiding amongst the shadows as they go,
Determined to take a 'shepherd's hut'
From a frail old lady of 94 or so.

Pickup attached ready to pull,
Wheels refuse to budge at all,
Crack as the axle bolts begin to snap,
Wheels tip inwards and gradually fall.

Signs of panic start to set in,
Element of surprise has all but gone,
This old hut is refusing to stir!
Mindless people have now moved on.

Relief of its owner the following day
Distressed by worry and fright,
Sleepless times for days to come,
What might happen another night?

Sybil's hut, now in safe hands
Away from uncertainty or strife,
Lovingly restored in new surroundings,
Ageing peacefully in her new life.

Rollin

It is perhaps a good opportunity at this stage of the book to take a step back in time to the 19th century, and include details of the Farris family in order to give a broader insight to the historical significance of my hut discovery.

The following updated article (and family pictures) have been included with the kind permission of George Farris's granddaughter, Sybil, and great granddaughter, Angela, to include in my book.

The History of the Coombe Bissett Steam Plough Works

Sybil's hand written history

by Sybil

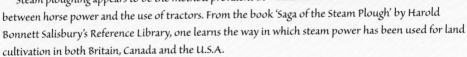

Introduction

This is the story of an enterprising and hard working Victorian family and their agricultural business efforts at a time in history when horses were being replaced by machines and when steam ploughs had been invented.

Steam ploughing appears to be the method prevalent in between horse power and the use of tractors. From the book 'Saga of the Steam Plough' by Harold Bonnett Salisbury's Reference Library, one learns the way in which steam power has been used for land cultivation in both Britain, Canada and the U.S.A.

Fowler's Steam Ploughing Apparatus appears to be the main British invention by a Wiltshire man who was born in Melksham in 1826, of a Quakers family. He died in 1864. He won the £500 prize for developing ploughing by steam power at the Dumfries Agricultural Show in 1857 and his 'Leeds Steam Plough Works' exhibited in the Paris Exhibition of 1855.

Thus the scene was set, by 1869, for the three brothers Charles, John and George Farris of Tollard Royal, to capitalise on this new agricultural invention.

The Farris family who founded the Coombe Bissett Steam Plough Works

Their story starts when Thomas Faris (born 1812) married Keturah Fanner of Tarrant Gunville, presumably at the church in that village. Her father owned the horse drawn carrier/bus service business between Blandford and Salisbury, now the 184 Wilts and Dorset bus service! They lived in Tollard Royal in the house next to the King John Hotel and which is still occupied and where Thomas had his adjoining works in agricultural ironmongery. Pieces of his manufacture are occasionally found.

They had nine children between the years of 1835 and 1851, but Thomas appears to have become restless, and wanting to shed the responsibility of his large family he disappeared to America leaving Keturah to face the hazardous future on her own. There is a lurid story that she had tried to follow her husband to America, and in the hotel bedroom, on the night prior to his embarkation, she awoke to find him standing over her with a knife in his hand; she screamed, he escaped, and that's the last that was heard of Thomas Faris.

In the 1861 Tollard Royal Census, Keturah is living at 70 Tollard Street and she described herself as a widow of 48 years of age. There are seven of the children still living with her, ranging in age from Charles aged 25 years to Louisa aged 9 years. The name now appears with two 'R's i.e. Farris. Keturah lived to be 94 years old.

Charles, the eldest son, was now in charge of his absent father's agricultural machinery business in Tollard Royal and on whom Keturah must have depended heavily. By 1875 he had established another foundry in Shaftesbury, as in the 1875 Shaftesbury Directory, he is described as 'Agricultural Implement Maker' of Haimes Lane and in 1881 the firm had a stand at the Royal Show in Salisbury.

Charles was obviously an ambitious entrepreneur as he then planned to expand the business to Coombe Bissett and he bought 'Picked Cawden' the 22 acre site in Salisbury Road where Old Foundry Cottage still stands. He planned to build the foundry works, plus six worker's cottages, plus a house for the family. Brothers John (aged 38) and George (aged 32) had joined in this new venture and the works were built in the late 1870's and machinery installed; the best of its kind: sawmills to be run by engines outside the building, carpentry equipment, lathes, furnaces and forges for blacksmith work etc, and several sets of engines and ploughs for steam ploughing had been bought.

Then tragedy struck - in 1879 Charles, aged 44, and Keturah's right-hand man, was thrown from his horse and killed on the zig-zag, when journeying from Tollard Royal to Shaftesbury works. Thomas, Keturah's third son then took over the management of the two foundries. This left the new enterprise at Coombe Bossett, in it's infancy, to brothers John and George. Only two of the workers cottages had been completed and plans for the other four cottages plus a house for the family were abandoned.

So John and George took over the management of the newly established foundry and steam plough works and the two young families lived in the semi-detached cottages.

However, a further tragedy happened in that John had left a loaded gun available for his small son to pick up and he accidentally killed George's six year old son Henry. John was severely reprimanded by the Salisbury Coroner for his negligence in leaving a loaded gun where there were children. A family row ensued resulting in John's departure, with his family, to manage the Shaftesbury and Tollard Royal foundries.

So George remained as the sole proprietor of the Coombe Bissett works, with his wife Harriet and their expanding family. He employed many local men and each steam ploughing tackle needed a team of five men plus a man to drive the horse drawn water barrel for the engines. In the works, much agricultural equipment was made - shepherds' houses to be taken on to the downs at lambing time (and cosy accommodation they were!), ploughs, hen houses and all agricultural needs of the day. The works were self- sufficient and their products were displayed in front of the works by the roadside. In the 1930's there was also a hand - operated petrol pump - surely the only petrol pump ever to be installed in Coombe Bissett.

George Farris sold his machinery at Salisbury market, his stand being next to the cheese market in the position of the present library. Horses were kept in his large paddock for family transport and to take goods to market.

He cultivated and harvested crops on his 22 acre land and his hobbies were shooting, shooting parties and making cider from his cider apple orchard. The family must have been practically self-supporting with produce from the land, a cow, a pig and chickens, plus rabbits in plenty in the fields, and the well for the water which supplied all needs from about 1882 (which seems to be the date when the cottages were first occupied) until mains water was installed in the 1930's. Now, in 1999, the well water level has been regularly checked and is found to be practically nil. The family enjoyed many outings to the Larmer Tree activities at Tollard Royal (e.g. gardens created in 1880 for public enjoyment by General Pitt Rivers) and the boys sang in Coombe Bissett choir and were bell ringers.

When George Farris was about sixty he became crippled with rheumatoid arthritis and used a donkey drawn wheelchair to convey him around the works and to inspect his crops. He died in 1924 and is buried in Coombe Bissett churchyard. George's widow, Harriet, and his youngest son Charlie (not yet born when the attached family photo was taken) carried on the business until 1931 when Harriet died. They had an office-showroom in Brown Street, Salisbury, entitled H & C Farris.

Steam ploughing seems to have been phased out after WW1. One relative remembers having seen it in use during WW1. Farming was in the doldrums in the early 1920's and, as the corn acreage grew smaller and fewer sheep kept on the downs and needing shepherds' houses, there was less work for the Farris firm and less sets of ploughing tackle were in use. But shepherds' houses were still in use until the 1930's and poultry houses needed for hens to be kept safely out in the stubble.

One of George Farris's sons complained that his father had wasted so much money on unsuccessful inventions. Nevertheless, there was still plenty of work for the Coombe Bissett firm as maintenance work on farm machinery and tractors was increasing.

And so, in 1931, when Charlie Farris married and established his own house and works on Coombe Hill, the Coombe Bissett Steam Plough Works, as such, ground to a halt, the building was

Back row *(left to right) Tom (eldest son), George Farris (Sybil's grandfather), Charles's wife (George's eldest brothers wife, from Berwick, St John, who used to live in the house after her husband's riding accident, and helped look after the children), Cousin.*
Middle row *(left to right) Uncle Jim, Cissie (Mary Ann, eldest daughter), Flo, Harriet (George's wife), Auntie Con (Constance), Auntie Susie.*
Front row *(left to right) Togo (George's dog), Uncle Walt (Walter), George (Sybil's father). Photograph taken at Coombe Bissett Foundry. Photo courtesy of Sybil Spinks (S.K.S).*

occupied by various tenant tradesmen and was eventually blown down in a gale in the early 1960's. The two-way water pump is all that survives of the once thriving Coombe Bissett Steam Plough Works.

This history was written by George Farris's granddaughter, Sybil (nee Farris) in 1999. The Old Foundry Cottages have always been occupied by members of the family since 1882. Sybil's old cottage, 1 The Old Foundry, is now owned by a descendent of Charles Farris (1835 to 1879).

Canada

Sybil was born on 24th April, 1917, in Saskatchewan, Canada, and was the younger daughter of George and Sarah Farris. Her father, George, met Sarah (nee Dyke, from Fishponds, Bristol) who was an infant teacher at Coombe Bissett School, when he took his much younger brother to her classroom every morning. As Sybil's daughter, Angela says, 'romance blossomed and they eventually became engaged'.

George Farris senior did not pay his sons a living wage, and when they wanted to marry, they had no choice but to leave the foundry in order to make an affordable income. George had heard from another relative, Walter, in 1910, who had gone to Canada, that prospects were good over there. During this period, fit young men were being encouraged to go out to the colonies in order to find work to make a reasonable living to improve their prospects.

George therefore decided to follow Walter to Canada in 1910, to eventually work for the Saskatoon Hospital, and planned to earn enough money and then send for Sarah so that they could get married. He worked hard in the lumber camps producing timber and underwent many hardships due to the freezing conditions and threat of wolves. He also studied for his engineering exams, having to walk 24 miles there and also back at night across the prairie to Saskatoon University, where he took his exam, passing first class. On one such occasion, the wolves closed around him at night on the way home, and he had to break in through a window of a trappers bothy to escape from them.

Two years later, Sarah did eventually emigrate to Canada, leaving her teaching job in Hilperton School, Wiltshire. Crossing the Atlantic by boat from Bristol would probably have been a worrying and somewhat apprehensive experience, as it was only three months after the Titanic sank. The day she arrived in Saskatoon, 12th July, 1912, George and Sarah were married after the evensong service in Saskatoon Church. One of the two volunteering witnesses present was called Sybil, who remained Sarah's life-long friend. George and Sarah named their second daughter, Sybil, after her, who in later years became the proud owner of one of her grandfather's pretty, portable huts. Sybil's second name is Kate. Their first daughter, Margery, was born in 1914 and died in the autumn of 2011, aged 98 years.

Sybil's mother missed England and disliked the extremes of temperature in Canada, so eventually left for England with George and their children, Margery and Sybil, on 24th April 1920 (Sybil's birthday). 'Aunty Biddy' arrived at Saskatoon CP Railway Station and gave her goddaughter, Sybil, a huge teddy for the week long journey, which is still treasured by the Farris family today. Sybil's daughter, Angela, visited Saskatoon in 2012 to retrace her grandparents footsteps over 100 years ago, and took Sybil's old teddy with her for the adventure, which is now displayed in Saskatoon Museum.

Dear David

Thank you for purchasing a copy of my book.

Best Wishes.

[signature]

Email:rollinspublications@gmail.com
Web:sybilshutbook.wix.com/sybilshut

Sybil's Hut

A history & appreciation of
Farris Shepherds' Huts
of the Coombe Bissett Steam Plough Works

Rollin Nicholls

The Farris Family Tree

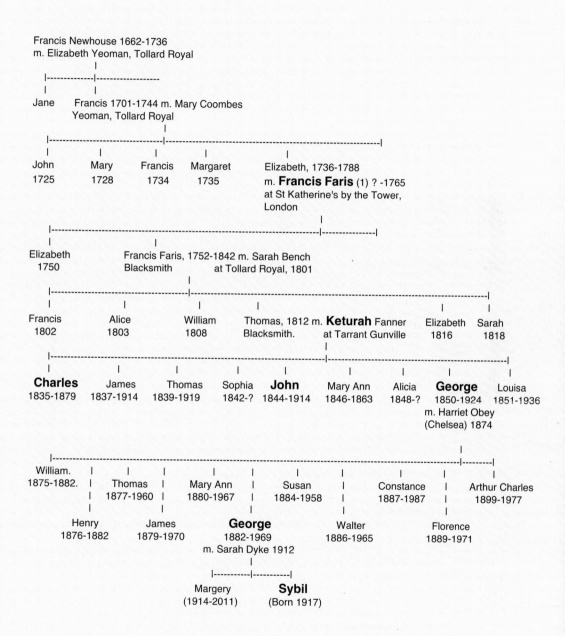

```
Francis Newhouse 1662-1736
m. Elizabeth Yeoman, Tollard Royal
                |
|--------------|--------------------
|              |
Jane       Francis 1701-1744 m. Mary Coombes
           Yeoman, Tollard Royal
                    |
|---------------------------------|-------------------------------------------------|
|             |            |          |
John        Mary       Francis    Margaret     Elizabeth, 1736-1788
1725        1728        1734       1735         m. Francis Faris (1) ? -1765
                                                at St Katherine's by the Tower,
                                                London
                                                        |
|-----------------------------------------------------------------|--------------|
|                            |                                                    |
Elizabeth              Francis Faris, 1752-1842 m. Sarah Bench
1750                       Blacksmith           at Tollard Royal, 1801
                                    |
|------------------------------|--------------------------------------------------------------------|
|               |              |            |              |                          |          |
Francis       Alice        William     Thomas, 1812 m. Keturah Fanner     Elizabeth   Sarah
1802          1803         1808        Blacksmith.      at Tarrant Gunville   1816        1818
                                                            |
|---------------------------------------------------------|-------------------------------------|
|             |            |            |            |            |          |          |          |
Charles      James      Thomas     Sophia      John     Mary Ann    Alicia    George    Louisa
1835-1879   1837-1914  1839-1919  1842-?    1844-1914  1846-1863   1848-?    1850-1924  1851-1936
                                                                             m. Harriet Obey
                                                                             (Chelsea) 1874
                                                                                    |
                                                                                    |--------|
|--------------------------------------------------------------------------------------|
William.   |        |        |          |          |          |          |          |        |
1875-1882. |      Thomas   |        Mary Ann    |        Susan       |      Constance  |    Arthur Charles
           |      1877-1960 |        1880-1967   |        1884-1958   |      1887-1987  |      1899-1977
           |        |        |          |          |          |          |          |        |
        Henry      James            George              Walter            Florence
        1876-1882  1879-1970        1882-1969           1886-1965         1889-1971
                                    m. Sarah Dyke 1912
                                         |
                                |-----------|-----------|
                              Margery         Sybil
                             (1914-2011)    (Born 1917)
```

NB: Francis Faris 1 (Number 1 is reference to the first time Faris appears)

Reminiscing with Sybil

During Christmas 2011, I was feeling very inspired as I had recently met Sybil and bought her hut from her. She had obviously made a huge impression on me so I started to write down the story of how I discovered the hut and after introducing myself to her, eventually purchased it. What really impressed me was the sheer enthusiasm and generosity given to me, from both Sybil and Angela. I was made to feel incredibly welcome, and was almost lost for words when I was presented with some of their family history and photographs. By January 2012, my story was starting to progress, and the flame for researching the history of Farris was ignited. I was hooked!

On a number of occasions during 2012, I visited Sybil at the Coombe Bissett cottages. Sybil relaxed in her chair, in her grandfather, George Farris's old cottage, and discussed different aspects of her family history in relation to the earlier years at Coombe Bissett. The following information includes snippets of additional facts not necessarily included in her hand written article about the history of the Coombe Bissett Steam Plough Works, which should be of interest to both collectors and enthusiasts of Farris shepherds' huts.

The Farris family tree (carefully checked by Sybil) has been included and is useful reference when reading both Sybil's article and reminiscences about her family's past.

Sybil thought that one of the most interesting persons in the family tree was Francis Faris (one 'r'), who died in 1765. He was a Persian man who had accompanied some horses of Arab bloodstock to this country.

He married Elizabeth (1736 to 1788) from Tollard Royal. Elizabeth was youngest daughter of Francis (1708 to 1744) and Mary Coombes. They met and married at St Katherine's by the Tower in London. Sybil said 'he must have been very in love with Elizabeth, as he gave up his job, religion, and family and adopted the family Christian name of Francis and retained his own surname of Faris, in order to marry her'. They had two children, Elizabeth, born 1750, and Francis (1752 to 1842).

The latter Francis (born in 1752) actually started the blacksmith business at Tollard Royal, Homington, and married Sarah. They had six children. Thomas, their middle son, born in 1812, married Keturah, born in 1813, and they continued a successful blacksmith business at the Tollard Royal premises. Unfortunately, Thomas decided to one day catch a train to Southampton and disappeared to America. Sybil's article on the Steam Plough Works history elaborates on this tale, with the lurid story of Thomas standing over his wife with a knife.

Keturah's eldest son, Charles, (1835 to 1879) continued the business in his father's absence, and married one of the Talbots, which brought money into the family. The story proceeds with Charles's tragic riding accident and continues with two of his brothers, John and George Farris, taking over the management of the

Picture: c.1880, of Kentura with her children at Tollard Royal. **Back row;** *Sophia, Mary Ann, John Farris (standing), Alicia, a relative.* **Front row;** *Louisa, Kentura, George Farris (sitting). Photo S.K.S.*

Coombe Bissettt Works together, until the shooting accident of George's son Henry (age five years eight month) in 1882. Sybil did indicate how the shooting accident happened, and one can only imagine the scene at the time.

The same year also saw the death of another of George and Harriet's sons, William (1875 to 1882) who unexpectedly died of pneumonia. The year 1882 had certainly been a memorable year for the Farris family, as the shooting accident happened when Harriet (Sybil's grandmother) was recovering from the birth of George (Sybil's father) in July 1882.

Sybil also commented that 'the cottages were built sometime during the late 1870's, as Charles who financed it died in 1879. They (George and John) seem to have occupied the cottages in 1882'.

As we know the foundry and cottages were built during the late 1870's, and the two brothers had occupied the Coombe Bissett cottages during 1882, this does give a good indication that production of Farris's earlier shepherds' houses could have been during the early 1880's, if not slightly before.

Due to the court case, family row, and obvious stress of the shooting incident, Sybil said that John only lived in the cottage alongside George at Coombe Bissett for

a few months, then eventually moved to Shaftesbury, where he set up his own business as Agricultural Implement Makers, probably working in Charles's already established works.

During one of our conversations, Sybil mentioned that George went bankrupt in 1902, but didn't lose his house and the premises, as he didn't actually own them. His elder brother, Charles, had originally bought the land. Sybil was certainly amused when I told her my research indicated that this was declared in the 1902 Edinburgh Gazette, November 18th, 1902. She felt that the reason for this was that it was so embarrassing that it was best to advertise the bankruptcy as far away as possible, and hope people would not notice!

Having discussed the topic of distribution agents with Sybil, it appears that her grandfather, George Farris, was very unlikely to have ever used an agent for the Coombe Bissett Steam Plough Works as 'he wouldn't want a middle man taking any of the profits'. She also remarked that 'George took orders for his huts from farmers at Salisbury market, as well as from passing trade at Coombe Bissett'.

George Farris senior died in 1924, and was buried at the church in Coombe Bissett. His eldest son, Thomas (born 1877), had started working in the business from the young age of 14 years until he was 19 years old. He volunteered to fight in the Boer War, and then became a successful gold miner. Sybil said that 'when Thomas was on holiday in Coombe Bissett, in the year his father died, he took everything'. As his father, George, had not made a will, and didn't technically own the house and land, he went and saw a solicitor, and secured both the land, premises and cottages in his name. He then charged his mother, Harriet, rent.

To complicate matters, George's youngest son Charles (or 'Charlie') had taken over the running of the business with his mother Harriet (H & C Farris) when his father, George, had died, and was also charged rent by his brother, which he found difficult to afford.

Sybil said that 'Harriet and Charlie lived together in her part of the semi. I don't know who lived next door then. Uncle Jim and Auntie Frances lived in that side for years before the family row of 1924, when Tom took everything. In the 1950's, Tom's daughter, Florrie lived there, coming from South Africa, until she died about 1986'.

Another brother, Uncle Jim (James 1879 to 1970) lived in John's cottage whilst his father was alive, and stayed with his father the longest. Sybil says he had a threshing machine business and towed behind his steam engine his threshing machine and tackle, and a George Farris shepherd's hut. The hut comprised of a bunk bed for Jim

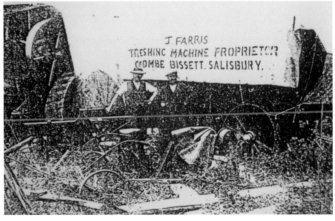

Above: Uncle Jim alongside a Marshall threshing drum. An elevator is in the foreground and a Wallis steam engine is behind. Photo S.K.S.

Right: An interesting picture shows Uncle Jim (on the left looking at the photo) displaying some of his implements and equipment. The banner above says 'J Farris Threshing Machine Proprietor Coombe Bissett Salisbury'. J Farris, in this instance, is for James Farris (not John Farris of Shaftesbury). Photo S.K.S.

and his helper to sleep in and also a stove. He would stay for a week at each farm (if a long distance from Coombe Bissett) in the hut and would take a weeks supply of food as well. Sybil recalls her aunty Francis preparing the food for him to take and commented 'How the meat survived in the hot climate whilst he was away, I will never know'. She had a long chuckle at the memory.

When Harriet died in 1931, Charlie decided to marry his sweetheart Nelly, from Coombe Farm. Sybil commented that 'Thomas decided at this time to double the rent to his brother, so Charles felt it was time to move on. Luckily, Nelly's father gave them some land to build their own house and workshop at Blandford Road, Coombe Hill'.

1924, Uncle Jim with pipe.
George (Sybil's father) sitting next to Jim.
Uncle Tom (sitting between the two ladies).
Photo S.K.S.

Sadly, the Coombe Bissett Steam Plough Works ground to a halt, as did the production of their shepherds' huts, and the premises were subsequently leased to various tenants, such as the car mechanic shop.

Sybil distinctly remembers when the company finished at Coombe Bissett, as she had a driving accident on the Blandford Road a year later. The man who was operating a car mechanic workshop at the Coombe Bissett premises came and collected the car and repaired it.

Sybil also recollected that there used to be a petrol pump near the road. After 1924, when a customer rang a hand bell, Auntie Susie would go and pump petrol into their vehicle for them.

Charlie Farris (youngest son of George senior) had now moved the business, H & C Farris, to Coombe Hill, Coombe Bissett, near Salisbury, and eventually continued with his young son, Hedley. Sybil said the business was more of a 'garage enterprise', and does not recall them making shepherds' huts there. The business imported combine harvesters from Canada, Australia and the USA, and set up a foundry during the Second World War to produce replacement parts for them. Trading ceased in the late 1980's. Hedley Charles Farris died on the 26th March 2011.

H&C Farris, Royal Counties Show 1948. Photo S.K.S.

It is certainly worth glancing at the family tree when reading about my discussions with Sybil, as it did start to become a little confusing at times, as she was quick on both names and dates, which is amazing at her age. There certainly appeared to be a lot of Francis's, John's, and Elizabeth's in the conversation. Sybil's father is called George, which took me a few moments to distinguish between Sybil's father, and George Farris, her grandfather, who was Proprietor at the Coombe Bissett Steam Plough Works.

It is also interesting that three of George's elder brothers, James (1837 to 1914), Thomas (1838 to 1919) and John Farris (1844 to 1914), all died in their later years around the time of the First World War. His eldest brother Charles (1835 to 1879), whom Sybil describes as an 'ambitious entrepreneur', had died years before in a riding accident, when thrown from his horse on the Shaftesbury zig zag.

Sybil also recalls her grandfather George making strong cider and inviting friends over for a drink. She couldn't contain her amusement when she said 'the

guests went home on the pony and trap, and the pony would find its way home and put itself back into its stable during the early hours of the morning, when the last guest had been deposited'. The pony was called Blackie and lived in the paddock at the rear of the foundry. Sybil recalls the pony and trap being used to collect her from the bus station when visiting Salisbury, during the period when she was six to ten years old.

Togo was George's dog and can also be seen in the old Farris family photo *(page 23)*. Sybil commented that sometimes he was kept chained by the outside toilet and slept in an open oak beer barrel. He was used as a gun dog as George had shooting parties.

A pony and trap with Harriet Farris & her youngest daughter Florence (Sybil's Aunty Flo) & Blackie the pony. It's just possible to see the Coombe Bissett foundry in the background. Photo S.K.S.

It appears that there was still a Farris shepherd's hut remaining outside the old foundry till the late 1950's as Angela has fond memories of playing in it as a child.

As Sybil mentioned in her history of the Coombe Bissett Works, the corrugated premises were blown down in a gale in the early 1960's. The house, however, was occupied by Cissie (eldest daughter Mary Ann) and her husband, Uncle Bob, for thirty years.

Sybil subsequently moved into George's cottage in 1994.

Farris Time line (including Sybil)

The following time line (checked by Sybil) shows where she stands in the family tree.

Thomas Farris (Born 1812 Blacksmith) married Keturah Fanner
(Sybil's great grandparents)
/

Charles Farris (1835-1879) – John Farris (1844-1914) – George Farris (1850-1924)
  (Sybil's great uncle)   (Sybil's great uncle)   (Sybil's grandfather)
/

Charles continued the agricultural business in Tollard Royal
Established a new foundry in Haimes Lane, Shaftesbury
Started Coombe Bissett Works
/

1879 Charles died in a riding accident
 Thomas (Keturah's third son) managed the foundries in Tollard Royal & Shaftesbury
/

1882 John & George Farris managed the Coombe Bissett Steam Plough Works
/

1882 Shooting accident – John Farris departed
/

George Farris continued at Coombe Bissett
/

1891 Census; *John & family living in Shaftesbury. Registered as an Implement maker at Tollard Royal. Sometime around the late 1880's and early 1900's, trading as J. Farris, Belle Vue Works, Shaftesbury, making shepherds' huts & agricultural implements. Registered in 1895 as an Implement maker at Belle Vue Works, Shaftesbury. Now trading as J. Farris & Sons. Ceased trading in 1975.*
/

1902 Coombe Bissett Works went bankrupt
/

Business continued to trade at the same premises
/

1910 George Junior (Sybil's father, born 1882) emigrated to Canada
/

1917 Sybil born (24th April)
/

1920 Sybil returned to England (aged 3 years)
/

1924 George Farris senior died
/

Harriet (George's widow) and Charlie continued to run the business (H & C Farris)

/

Thomas (George's eldest son) took over the ownership of the Coombe Bissett premises

/

1931 Harriet died

Charlie married Nelly & moved to Blandford Road, Coombe Hill & started a new enterprise that ceased trading in the 1980's

/

Coombe Bissett Works ceased trading – Premises leased to tenants

/

1960's Premises blown down in a gale

/

1994 Sybil moved to the Foundry Cottages

/

2002 Sybil's hut discovered & returns home (after 100 years) to the original George Farris Coombe Bissett Steam Plough Works site

/

2011 Sybil's hut sold & entrusted to the author of this book to preserve for future generations to enjoy

Old postcard of Coombe Bissett

Coombe Bissett Steam Plough Works layout

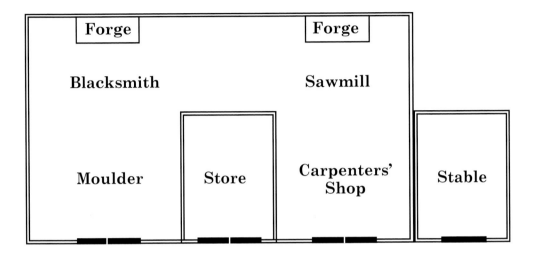

Layout of the Coombe Bissett Steam Plough Works.

Sybil kindly gave me a floor plan of the original foundry layout and a drawing of how the building would have looked during the 19th century. Although there are no measurements to accurately assess the overall size of individual areas, it is possible to determine the exact locations of individual work areas as well as the general appearance of the Coombe Bissett Works as a whole.

The floor plan shows where the two forges were positioned, as well as the location of the blacksmith, moulder, sawmill and carpenters' shop, plus the store and stables. Over the years, George relied on his sons to help in the business alongside a few local employees, although, as previously mentioned, not all of his sons, such as Sybil's father, could afford to continue working with him.

The foundry cottages are still located alongside the A 354, on the Coombe Bissett to Salisbury road. The works premises were situated at the top of the bank at the north eastern side of the cottages, close to where Sybil kept her hut.

The outline of the Coombe Bissett Steam Plough Works appears to be marked on some late 1890's and early 1900's maps of Coombe Bissett and Homington. It's worth investigating, as it's sometimes possible to see the

Sketch of the Coombe Bissett Steam Plough Works. S.K.S.

location of the cottages and the corrugated workshop, with some examples actually stating 'Coombe Bissett Steam Plough Works'. Now and then, maps with good detailing of the foundry might be discovered, which includes the drive that curves in front of the workshop, with a separate entrance and exit onto the A 354.

As a guide, look for one of the footpaths from Homington House that leads towards the Coombe Bissett to Salisbury road. The foundry cottages and workshop were situated on the opposite side of the road.

Maps that include the original foundry are increasingly becoming hard to find, especially in decent condition, and are certainly worth collecting and framing, thereby providing additional historical evidence and memorabilia for a Farris collection.

Steam ploughing

Steam engines for ploughing were a crucial asset for the Coombe Bissett Steam Plough Works as they contributed to an important part of their business, along with their foundry and workshop, where they built their shepherds' huts. Sybil mentioned in her article about the Fowlers Steam Ploughing Apparatus and how the Farris brothers capitalised on this invention.

There were, however, other early influential inventors of steam ploughing, such as John Heathcoat, Lord Willoughby d'Eresby and John T. Osborn, to name but a few, whose early inventions and designs in improvements to drainage and cultivation machinery indirectly contributed towards Fowler's success.

John Fowler became an accomplished agricultural engineer and inventor, being awarded numerous agricultural prizes and awards during the mid to late 19th century, for demonstrating the practicability and profitability of his cable cultivation system. Fowler had developed three distinct systems. two of them incorporating a steam engine and numerous anchors (or windlass) with pulleys and steel cables. However, his most successful apparatus consisted of two steam engines being used to pull ploughs across a field from one side to the other. His invention is renowned for reducing the cost of ploughing farmland due to its increased efficiency to the horse and plough, as it was quicker, caused less compaction to the soil (e.g. by horses) and was not so reliant on weather conditions.

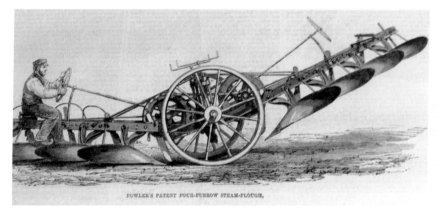

Print of an engraving from The Illustrated London News (1862).

FOWLER'S PATENT FOUR-FURROW STEAM-PLOUGH.

The basic principle of steam ploughing:

Fowlers original and best invention appears to have consisted of two steam traction engines, one either side of the field, that dragged a plough across with steel cables that were located on a winding drum underneath the engine. His use of a wheeled 'balanced' plough, which was basically two ploughs in one, on a see-saw iron frame, consisting of a left handed implement on one end and a right handed implement on the other end, proved invaluable to his success.

Steam ploughing at The Great Dorset Steam Fair. Photo J.L.

As the plough was pulled across the field, the front end would tip upwards, like a see-saw, whilst the other end, with the operator sitting on it, would produce a furrow. On reaching the steam engine that had pulled it across the field, the process would be reversed, and the operator would then sit on the other end of the plough which would now produce a furrow, as the opposite end, which had previously created a furrow, would then see-saw upwards (or balance in the air), to return to the other steam engine. The steam engines would gradually move forward, one furrow at a time, and communicate via their engine whistles.

Steam ploughing was very labour intensive and time consuming. Steam engines would need coal and water and could easily take a couple of hours to heat up to produce enough steam. Ideally, a team of around five men would be necessary to run the engines, ploughs and tackle. The engines usually pulled a living van to sleep in, a water cart for the steam engines, as well as ploughs and implements, as the team moved between jobs.

Sybil remarked that 'George hired out five sets of steam ploughs to farmers', which would have been a huge financial outlay in those days. The cost of a steam plough would easily have reached a few thousand pounds. Additional costs, such as the ploughs and steel cable, also needed to be accounted for.

Other influential companies such as Aveling and Porter of Rochester, Charles Burrell & Sons of Norfolk and J. F. Howard of Bedford, were all reputable British builders of steam engines and agricultural machinery that helped contribute towards steam ploughing in general during the 19th century. As steam ploughs and apparatus became widespread, modifications and improvements were implemented, providing a variety of choices and designs for farmers and contractors to use.

Sounds of the Night

There's a distant sound in the night,
The shepherd stirs in his hut
And grunts with delight,
As he fumbles for his lantern.

There are new born lambs to feed,
He must soon go outside
And attend their every need,
He leaves the warmth of his stove.

Slowly, he opens the wooden door,
He feels a cool breeze on his face
And can hear the sound no more,
As he climbs down the steps.

With his curiosity starting to grow,
Eyes straining into the darkness,
Candle making a flickering glow,
He clasps his crook in anticipation.

There is movement on the ground,
Faces appear from the shadows,
Eyes stare motionless from all around,
His sheep are close by and all is well!

The shepherd works all night long,
His kindness never dwindles,
As birds sing a cheerful song
Amongst their morning chorus.

The work is exhausting and tough,
His flock always reliant and assured,
The life he leads can be rough,
But the rewards are immense.

There is nature all around him,
Some folk envious of his outdoor life,
When the weather is a little grim
He takes refuge in his shepherd's hut.

Welcome shelter on the downs,
A little rustic around the edges,
Step inside and listen to the sounds,
That a shepherd enjoys all his life!

Rollin

One of the earlier poems that I wrote, depicting the life
of a shepherd with his sheep and hut.

Sybil's Hut Construction Details & Farris Shepherds' Houses

On closer inspection of Sybil's hut, it soon became apparent it was different to the usual George Farris shepherds' houses and had been originally built as a portable granary (or grain store). Angela confirmed this when I purchased it, and had previously got independent expert advice to clarify it, although she said she and her mum would always think of it as a shepherd's hut. I have also inspected it with hut expert and enthusiast, Eddie Butterfield of Butterfield Ironworks, Bere Regis, who also came to the same conclusion that it was actually built as a granary.

A Farris portable granary was not intended to be used by shepherds to live in during lambing time. It was constructed as a simple mobile hut that was used to store sacks of threshed grain in around the farm, thereby giving some protection from poor weather conditions as well as from rodents such as rats. They could also be used for storing animal feed, produce and general farming equipment if required.

During the late 19th century, mechanical threshing enabled stems and husks of plants to be loaded by hand into a machine, powered by a steam engine, which automatically separated grain or seeds from the straw, which was subsequently used for bedding, or run through a reed comber for thatching material. Grain was distributed into hessian sacking and was then usually loaded and transported on a horse drawn cart for storage on the farm, or at a mill. Once the grain arrived at the farm, it could be loaded into a granary for storage purposes.

A granary would generally have been used as a storage facility rather than for carrying heavy loads. Their mobility however, would have provided a degree of flexibility of use, making them useful additions throughout the seasons.

Interestingly, one of John Farris's great grandsons confirmed his great grandfather also made smaller huts suitable for storing sacks of grain, and suggested their larger shepherds' huts had slightly 'flatter' curved roofs.

First impressions, one would surmise Sybil's granary is a shepherd's hut. There are subtle differences which are outlined in the following chapters. Whilst writing this book, Sybil's hut has also been referred to as a granary as that is what it actually is! Reference to a portable granary can usually be found in late 19th to early 20th century manufacturers adverts and price lists.

The terms shepherds' huts (or houses) has generally been reserved in this book for examples that were mainly used for shepherds to live in. Shepherds' huts and shepherds' houses are names that were often used in period catalogues, magazines and adverts to describe these mobile living spaces for use on the downs. Shepherds' lambing huts and shepherds' wagons are also phrases synonymous with these portable houses.

The following in depth construction details and observations give an insight into the obvious and more subtle differences and comparisons between an uncommon George Farris portable granary and their shepherds' houses. Although it should be

*The interior of
Sybil's granary
showing period tools
and implements.*

40

interesting and useful information for an enthusiast and hut restorer, hopefully it won't be too tedious and laborious for others. Please read on!

It should be noted that huts built by Farris over the years would have had some minor, individual differences, as they were hand built, and may have also been altered slightly to suit customers requirements and preferences. Some comparisons in design are also made between George Farris's examples and his brother (and competitor) John Farris.

Hut Sizes

Sybil remarked that 'George Farris huts would have been of standard sizes'. My research of unrestored examples has shown that three sizes in particular appear consistent and the norm, although exceptions may exist.

Standard sizes.
G. Farris: 8ft x 6ft.
        10ft x 6ft.
        12 ft x 6ft.
Measurements are in imperial as originally used during their construction.

The smallest size was about 8ft long x 6ft wide externally. A sliding window and internal panelling in an example studied indicates it could have been used by a shepherd. A stove and flue was not fitted. It also had the same early rectangular name plate as Sybil's granary, and a narrow, central, internal roof support, curving across the ceiling. The axles were wooden. It is very probable that a more basic version, without internal panelling and window, could have been available to store grain in.

Sybil's portable granary is larger and measures approximately 10ft x 6ft externally (122 3/4" long x 73 1/2" wide) with internal ceiling height of 6ft 6" from the underside of the curved central roof beam to wooden floor. This beam interestingly is made from elm and measures 2 3/8" wide x 2 3/8" deep. A sliding window, stove, or wooden matchboard panelling, were not included, thereby reducing production costs and providing a cheaper option to the standard shepherd's hut construction.

George Farris however, also built huts the same size as Sybil's granary with internal panelling, small sliding window and wooden axles along the same lines as their shepherd's house specifications. An example investigated had an interesting history, being used by a shepherd for many years of its life, with evidence of sheep counting scribbled on its interior panelling, and later used as a pheasant shoot shelter.

George's larger huts were generally made as shepherds' houses and gave considerably more room when compared to their smaller designs, and would have often been purchased by farming estates who could afford a little more comfort and space for their shepherds. Evidence of stoves being installed is usually apparent. It is possible that some larger huts may originally have been produced as granaries, although there is little evidence of this.

An example with oblong name plate that has been measured was 12 1/4 ft x 6 1/2 ft externally (147" long x 78" wide). The height was 82" externally, from roof apex to wooden floor level, and about 114" from the apex to ground level, allowing for minor discrepancies with the ground surface. One could be forgiven in presuming that the overall exterior height of all Farris huts would be the same, but there are subtle differences between models as they are individually hand built.

Interestingly, my research on George's larger shepherds' houses indicates that they were usually a few inches longer and wider than his brother, John's, examples, some of which are included in this book.

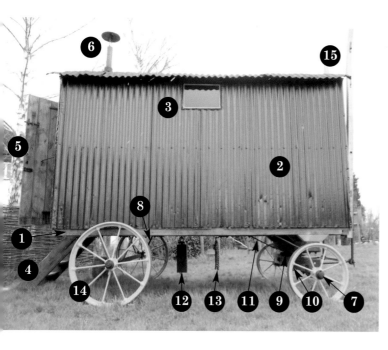

1. Wooden chassis.
2. External corrugated sheeting *(side & curved roof panels).*
3. Window *(n/a granary).*
4. Wooden steps.
5. Wooden door.
6. Stove & flue *(n/a granary).*
7. Axle beams & stub axles.
8. Rear axle support braces *(location only).*
9. Turntable.
10. Front axle central support bar *(location only).*
11. Front axle side support braces.
12. Drag Shoe.*
13. Brake chain.*
14. Cast Wheels *(front & rear).*
15. Wooden horse shafts.
16. Interior matchboard panelling *(See page 44)*

NB. For purposes of clarification, the 'front' of the hut is the horse shafts end, whilst the 'rear' is where the door and steps are normally situated.
*N/a = not applicable. *Additional items.*

A typical shepherd's hut construction

A timber framework is constructed over a softwood timber chassis with galvanised corrugated sheeting used on the sides and roof. Strong axles, turntable (for steering), wheels and horse shafts enable movability of the construction. A wooden floor, door and steps are the other main requirements to complete the basic structure.

The inclusion of internal panelling, window and optional stove and flue would normally have been included if constructed as a shepherd's hut, rather than a more basic portable granary, in order to make it more comfortable and practical for shepherds during lambing time.

Chassis

Traditional shepherds' huts had chassis' that were of wooden construction. Farris produced theirs in a number of sizes and thicknesses to suit their various models. The type of timber used for the chassis and usually the axles, was a good quality seasoned softwood pine (e.g. Pinus species), which was strong and durable, and reasonably easy to work.

During the mid to late 19th century, a huge amount of timber was being imported from overseas by ships to numerous ports around Britain. Imported timber was commonly known as 'ships timbers'. Around this time, Poole harbour was extremely busy due to the development of Bournemouth, and with the eventual railway connection with Salisbury, it's very likely that some of the timber used by Farris could have originated from this source, rather than just supplied locally. George Farris was certainly having his corrugated sheeting supplied from Bournemouth via rail, which is briefly mentioned later on.

Factors such as availability and cost would have been two of the main influential considerations when choosing and purchasing materials for shepherds' huts. Period adverts of Timber Importers and Manufacturers generally show an array of woods available, such as ash, oak, birch, hickory, elm, whitewood and pine.

The introduction of the 1919 Forestry Act has contributed enormously over the years to the increase of sustainable timbers that are available for use in Britain these days. Managed conifer plantations have provided a substantial timber source such as Douglas Fir (Pseudotsuga menziesii) or Larch (Larix species) which are excellent timbers used today for replacement chassis parts and axles on original shepherds' huts, as well as new creations that are built in the traditional way.

Sometimes, oak axles are found on some Farris shepherds' huts (usually the front axles), but its probable that these may be replacement beams. One has a tendency to think oak is advantageous because it is a hardwood, but this can be outweighed by a number of disadvantages associated with this timber. For example, oak is more expensive than softwoods, is harder to work, and has a tendency to split over time. The tannins in the oak also tend to corrode the wrought iron axle bolts.

As with all Farris huts, the original wooden chassis on Sybil's granary is remarkably strong and consists of four sturdy parallel beams (also referred to as chassis members), measuring 3" x 4" deep, that supports the pine floor from front to rear.

Granary chassis timber sizes:

Length   120 1/2" X 3" x 4" deep.
Width.   72 3/8" X 3" x 4" deep.
(NB. 3 7/8" deep to be precise).

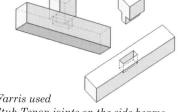

G. Farris used
a) Stub Tenon joints on the side beams
b) Mortice & Tenon joints on the middle beams

George Farris's wooden chassis' have stub tenon joints on the side beams where the outer timbers meet the corners, and mortice and tenon joints on the middle beams (e.g. the tenon is cut to fit the mortise hole).

As a comparison, early John Farris chassis' have mortise and tenon frame joints on all beams, and have a sturdy blacksmith made wrought iron strengthening strap in each corner, running vertically, that secures the body frame and chassis together. The positioning of these straps can vary slightly.

J. Farris used
Mortise &
Tenon joints.

The strengthening straps on J. Farris examples (e.g. circular name plate) have a section 6 3/4" long x 1 1/2" wide x 3/8" thick, visible on the inside of the hut. The length of the strap then extends through the floor and chassis member and is another 7", which comprises of a 1/2" bar that is threaded on the end to accept a bolt (total length 13 3/4"). The visible flat section inside the hut is secured with three screws, and the bar is fastened under the chassis by a washer and bolt. Slight variations in strap sizes are to be expected as they are hand forged. A few examples may also have evidence of the Farris name on the rear side if examined carefully.

Above: J. Farris (horseshoe name plate) panelled interior. Note the wrought iron body frame to chassis corner strengthening straps.

Some comparisons of George and John's chassis sizes are given in the 'Brief construction detailing at a glance' section later in the book.

Above: J. Farris wrought iron body frame to chassis strengthening strap.

Granary body construction

The outside of Sybil's granary is constructed of rounded galvanised, corrugated iron, which is normal on all Farris huts. This sheeting would probably have been painted with either lead paint, tar, or pitch, when originally built. Evidence of a thick tar can usually be found under the overlap of some old corrugated sheets, suggesting that an application of tar had been applied before fitting the panels into place.

Early corrugated sheets were made from wrought iron without being galvanised. Mild steel corrugation appears to have gradually replaced wrought iron sometime around the 1890's, so it's possible that the sheeting on some very early Farris huts could have consisted of wrought iron (which was brittle) rather than steel sheeting.

Interestingly, c.1900 period adverts state that galvanised corrugated sheets were used on shepherds' huts. Galvanising was important as it prevented deterioration of the corrugation, but an application of a product such as tar was useful for additional preservation and weatherproofing.

The width of the corrugated sheets are 26" and have an overlap of 2" giving 24" panels when fitted. A useful and quick way of estimating the size of a hut is by counting the number of sheets it has along its length and width. The height of the side panel sheeting measures 72 1/2" on the granary (e.g. approx. 6ft is usual for both George's and John's huts) and the curved roof sheeting is around 90" on all the huts that I have measured.

The granary corrugation is attached on the outside with early type 2 3/4" nails and washers. There are two different styles of nails that have been used. One has a large domed head and thickish flat washer (e.g. corrugated roofing nail), the other has a smaller head with a separate small domed washer, not dissimilar to modern spring head nails with a tiny head and larger domed washer. The large domed headed examples with a flat washer were also used on early John Farris examples.

George Farris also used a large slotted domed head threaded type with thickish flat washer on some of their later huts. Although they had a slotted head they were commonly hammered

Interior of granary with replacement front axle timbers.

Interior of restored granary with a collection of period tools and equipment.

into place. These are worth collecting if you ever see any available, as they are extremely useful when one needs to plug an oversized hole in the timber frame, or chassis, to secure the corrugated sheeting. A 'plug' can be inserted, and this later threaded type screwed in accordingly.

The interior of the granary has 1" wide x 1/8" thick additional galvanised metal strips running vertically on the inside, secured by galvanised 'domed' headed bolts (approx. 1/2" long) and square nuts, peened over on the ends, to strengthen the corrugation where the sheets overlap. This is most unusual for G. Farris huts, but probably felt necessary for the granary as there was no internal pine panelling to help stiffen and support the body. The exterior overlapping corrugated sheets were drilled, 1/4" thick bolts inserted through the sheets, including the drilled internal metal strips, and the adjacent corrugation was then 'sandwiched' between the outer sheet and internal strip before everything was bolted together. Two strips 35" long were used on each panel (70" total length) plus six nuts and bolts. The slotted head of the domed bolts measure 1/2" in diameter.

Included inside, against the corrugation, are the usual iron braces (1" wide x 3/8" thick) that run diagonally (one brace front & rear) and secured from the framework down to the chassis. George's huts are designed with these to help support the bodywork and reduce flexing when being towed by a horse. On panelled examples these braces are not hidden, and are situated in front of the panelling, but behind the central wooden beam that runs horizontally around the interior.

Additional 1" wide x 3/8" thick internal braces at the forward end of the side panels to support the framework to the floor were also included in the granaries design and are not usually present in the larger G. Farris shepherds' houses. These are also made from wrought iron, with hot diagonal punched square holes to take a coach bolt at either end.

The granary has interior body bracing rods (e.g. 3/8" thick iron rods threaded on each end) located inside the hut (forward and rear) and are positioned across the interior roof line and are attached through the wooden frame. Similar rods are also located under the floorboards and secured through the chassis with square nuts. These rods are usually 1/2" thick in larger huts. This is usual on all of George's models and helps to hold everything together. These threaded iron bracing rods and 1" wide internal braces do not appear to be included in John Farris huts.

Sybil commented that 'her grandfather bought corrugated sheeting for his huts from a Bournemouth firm, and had it delivered to Salisbury by train. He then collected it and brought it back to the foundry at Coombe Bissett'. Close inspection of the inside of the corrugated sheeting inside the granary confirmed she was correct as a 'delivery note' to Salisbury station is written on the inside on a couple of the corrugated roof panels and also on one of the side panels. More details are provided later when discussing 'evidence of the past'.

Other G. Farris shepherds' huts have also been known to provide similar evidence of a delivery note, usually discovered during a restoration when some of their internal matchboard panelling has been removed. It goes without saying that preservation of these sheets is essential in order to retain the historic importance associated with them!

Another unusual feature of the granary is an additional rough sawn wooden horizontal beam (2" x 3" deep) that is positioned below the usual planed timber beams (2" x 2 3/4" deep) that run centrally around the interior of a Farris hut. These planed central beams can vary in thickness in other Farris models. For example, one of George's shepherds' houses (e.g. oblong

Hooper & Ashby delivery note on the interior of the corrugated sheeting.

name plate) had a 2 3/4" x 3" deep beam, and one of John's early huts was found to have a beam 2" x 3" deep. Although quite narrow, they are very useful for placing small possessions on, such as sheep shears, shepherds salve pot, drenching horn, mug, tins, etc.

The granary also had a piece of wood supported across its interior width (at the front end, resting on these planed horizontal timbers), which provided a bed for Jim to sleep on when staying in it. A piece of old elm was eventually sourced and used (size 6ft x 2ft x 1" thick) as it looked more authentic and pleasing and was suitable for future storage and display purposes.

The height of the lower additional rough sawn beam in the granary may have been included to allow for extra support when leaning large heavy sacks of grain against the inside of the bodywork. The normal planed timber above also allowed for these larger type hessian sacks to be supported. However, the two beams together does allow for double stacking of smaller sacks. Their height (measured from the floor to the top part of the beams) are about 17" and 34" respectively. A simple but very useful and cost effective idea for extra support or double stacking of sacks.

It is probable that the additional rough beam would have had tenon joints if included in the huts original construction, as it has been attached to the internal framework with large nails. Early large type domed headed nails and washers, to hold the corrugation in place on the outside, have also been used to help secure this extra beam against the inside of the sheeting, which suggests it could have been included as an afterthought by Farris to improve the design.

The main framework inside the granary consists of planed vertical timbers (approx. 3" x 3") at each corner, horizontal timbers (2 3/4" x 2 3/4" deep) running just below the roof line along the sides, front and rear, as well as the middle horizontal beams that have already been mentioned. The framework is built onto a timber chassis and a timber floor was then nailed into position.

As a comparison, one of George's larger huts measured (with oblong name plate) had vertical corner timbers 3 1/4" x 2 3/4" thick, horizontal timbers below the roof line 3 1/4" wide x 3" deep, and a central beam running around the hut, roughly 2 3/4" wide x 3" deep, the latter having slight variations occurring on individual beams. It can be intriguing how variable the thickness of some timbers are, but perhaps it's not that surprising considering huts were individually hand built, and timbers would normally have been planed by hand before the introduction of basic belt driven planers.

Because there is no interior wooden panelling in Sybil's granary, condensation can sometimes occur. There is evidence, between the side corrugation and interior framework, of hessian being originally placed from the top horizontal beam down to the pine floor, probably in order to help reduce this problem, and also to provide some form of insulation. This could also signify that it could be quite an early example.

Sybil did remark that when Jim used to stay in her hut the floor would sometimes become wet, and this condensation problem would have been the reason. The original pine floor, however, has survived remarkably well, with only a few of the rear boards showing any serious signs of decay. There is also evidence of woodworm and a few areas where mice had been nibbling. Luckily there is no major damage caused by rats, which is one of the common problems associated with these rodents and portable granaries.

There are also indications of corrosion on the lower inner parts of the corrugation where the hessian had originally been sandwich between the floor and the sheeting, although its not too serious, and can be treated and preserved.

The width of the individual pine tongue and grooved floorboards are 5" in

Remnants of hessian & jottings inside the granary.

the granary which appears to be fairly consistent with some of the smaller huts examined. A small example thought to be built by John Farris was also found to have similar width floorboards. Larger shepherds' houses made by both George and John Farris usually had wider 6 1/2" floorboards. Original hardwood oak floors can also be discovered in some of George's larger huts, providing a more expensive but quality option.

Farris shepherds' houses are panelled on the inside with tongue and grooved pine matchboarding, but examples can sometimes be discovered without panelling on the ceiling. The exclusion of matchboarding on the ceiling was an option to help keep costs down and prices competitive. The width of the panels can also vary (e.g. 5 1/2" and 6 1/2") depending on the model. Generally speaking, George's smaller huts often had narrower panelling, whilst his larger ones tended to have wider boards.

However, the 'brief construction detailing' section later on in this book, does indicate that some of the larger shepherds' houses measured did sometimes have original narrow matchboarding, probably due to the availability of timber at the time of the huts construction, so variations are to be expected.

Insulation between the internal panelling and corrugated sheeting is not usually apparent in old shepherds' huts, but some insulation with horse hair between the external corrugated roof and the ceiling panelling has been found in an early unrestored John Farris restoration project.

The central wooden interior curved roof support on George Farris huts can vary in depth. As mentioned, Sybil's granary has quite a narrow curved elm support (2 1/2" x 2 1/2" deep), running across the width of the roof. The narrow depth is normal on

The granaries corrugated interior.

G. Farris (oval name plate) panelled interior.

J. Farris (horseshoe name plate) panelled matchboard interior with original sliding window.

George's earlier examples. Some of George's later shepherds' houses (e.g. oblong name plate) had deeper supports about 1 1/4" x 6" deep. John Farris huts usually have a characteristic heavy wrought iron curved interior roof support (1 3/4" x 1/2" deep) running across the width of the ceiling. However, I have also seen a couple of J. Farris & Sons examples with a curved wooden roof support with a narrow depth. The roof supports also help to hold the ceiling panelling in position when fitted.

The granary also has a long beam, measuring 121 1/2" long x 2 3/4" wide x 2" deep, running the length of the ceiling through the central curved support. Examples with deeper wooden roof supports (e.g. oblong name plate) usually had a thicker 2 3/4" wide x 3" deep beam, running along the middle of the ceiling from front to rear, although the thickness can vary slightly in some models. These internal timber beams run the length of the roof and are located (e.g. slightly channelled) into the wooden apex roof end boards at either end. The long ceiling beams are not applicable to curved wrought iron roof support designs in John's huts.

Windows

Sybil's granary has no small wooden sliding window as it was designed as a portable store for grain. Nevertheless, a window was essential in both George's and John's shepherds' houses to provide some natural light and ventilation, as well as observation of the sheep for the shepherd. Examples that require restoration may show remnants of a reddish stain on their small wooden window frames, which matches the original red colour sometimes found on the inside wooden panelling. Periodically the panelling was left polished and not stained. Windows are normally located on the offside of the hut just below the roof line. The positioning of windows can also vary slightly on some Farris examples.

George's windows tend to slide towards the front of the hut, whilst John's often slide towards the rear when opened. There no doubt will be exceptions.

Sliding windows measure in the region of 20" x 14 1/4" which gives an indication of how restrictive these windows were as far as light is concerned. Glass thickness was about 1/8" and was clear. The sliding method of the window is very basic. The timber framework which holds the glass slides between the internal panelling and a strip of beading (approx. 42 1/2" x 1 1/4" x 1/2" thick), was positioned top and bottom of the window frame.

When windows have been altered or enlarged over the years, the evidence of the small original sliding examples are sometimes apparent, where it has left scratches or small grooves in the adjacent wooden panelling, where it has rubbed when it has been opened and closed.

John's very early huts had a flat piece of thin metal cut roughly to the shape of the corrugated ribbing that was attached to the bottom section of the window frame. This acted as a very crude window sill that was only reasonably efficient in torrential rain. Subsequently, there was a tendency for water to seep in. Lead or galvanised 'sills' can sometimes be found attached to the lower window frame on some of John's early examples as an improvement or modification. George's sliding windows tend to have a wooden sill.

A view through an original J. Farris (circular name plate) small sliding window.

A small G. Farris (large rectangular name plate) shepherd's hut. Photo J.L.   53

Steps & Door

Attached to the rear chassis below the door entrance on Sybil's granary are two large wrought iron brackets (or eyes) to support the wooden steps. These early brackets are wider than later ones, although the exact size would also depend on the material available when forged. The position of the granary brackets had been altered to face downwards as the timber had started to split due to the regular use of the steps over the years. They should protrude outwards (e.g. horizontally) rather than downwards, and were originally located under the rear chassis member.

The granary step brackets measure 5" long overall, 2 1/2" across at their widest part, and 2" wide at their narrowest section, and have a central hole of 1 1/2" for the step securing hooks to locate into easily. The width of some later bracket ends are narrower, and are about 1 3/4" wide, with a 1" central hole, and about 5 1/2" long. The forged side securing hooks measure around 13" long (including 2" curve on the end that secures the steps in place) and 1" wide. Two side hooks are required, with one attached either side of the steps.

The original steps would have rotted years ago, and the example that came with the granary looked in reasonable condition, but on close examination, had not been made in a traditional softwood or hardwood (e.g. laminated wood had been used) and were very steep. They would definitely need replacing! It's not clear whether the ones included with Farris huts would have consisted of three or four steps, but it's probably more important to make a set that feels comfortable and easy to walk up and down.

I have seen some beautiful restorations, only to be spoilt by steps which were quite dangerous due to either the angle of them, or the closeness, or distance, between the individual planks that formed the steps to walk on. Damp or frosty steps are another

G. Farris later step bracket and hook.

problem to consider, and a hand rail may be
appropriate. Sometimes, unrestored huts can be
found with a hand rail attached to the nearside rear
door frame, but these usually appear to be later
additions included presumably for practical and
safety reasons.

A tall rustic stake firmly positioned alongside the
steps is a simple option that I use and provides a
degree of stability when climbing in and out of a hut.
I have even seen a piece of short rope attached to the
door pillar and used with some success. If some sort
of support is required, ensure it is sturdy enough
and safe to use.

Signs of old chicken mesh or even modifications
such as channelled grooves incorporated into
replacement steps, in order to help provide more
grip when walking up and down them, can be seen on
some examples. Again, safety of use is paramount if

*A hand rail provides a practical solution
when climbing in & out of a hut.*

considering any improvements in design, but generally speaking, most hut steps that
I've trundled up and down are pretty hazardous in wet or icy conditions, regardless of
attempts to make them safer.

Granary early step bracket & hook.

Steps measure about 26 1/2" wide. The overall height can vary slightly depending on factors such as:

1. The distance the chassis stands from ground level (e.g. are the correct Farris wheels fitted).
2. The location of the step brackets that are attached to the rear of the chassis.
3. The exact position of the side securing hooks that are attached to the steps.

The door of the granary had previously been renewed, but an old photograph of the original door confirms it was of the usual two piece stable door type, with the top half being slightly smaller than the bottom section. It is not uncommon to find huts with replacement doors, but where original doors are present, albeit rotten, it is preferable to make an exact copy if the old door is not restorable. The problem with this is that where the top opening section is smaller than the bottom part, the view when seated inside the hut can be restricted. Combined with a small window high up in the side panelling, which was normal with Farris shepherds' houses, ones view to the outside world is somewhat limited. This won't necessarily appeal to some owners who want to sit inside with the bottom half of the door closed, and look outside. To add to the restricted view, Farris huts were not supplied with a window in the door, but would have been fitted at the customers request if required.

Positioning of the rear door was commonly on the rear near side and was made of 6 1/2" tongue and groove pine. Door frames are usually around 68 1/2" high x 31" wide for both George's and John's shepherds' houses. A forged wrought iron hook, similar to horse shaft hooks, were the norm on all Farris huts to hold the door open and were usually attached to the bottom half of the door.

As they were blacksmith made, styles, thicknesses and sizes varied slightly, both on George's and John's models. The granary rear door hook is 6 3/4" long curving to an additional 2 1/2" where it secures onto the door and is 3/8" thick. As a comparison, the front hook for securing the horse shafts is 8 1/2" long curving to an additional 2" where it fastens onto the shafts. Both are located onto a 3/8" wrought iron bar (sometimes a 1/2" bar was used) with turned 'eye', which goes through the corrugated sheeting and interior timber frame. A square nut (and usually a washer) holds the bar in place.

The width of the wooden slats on the replacement granary door are a little narrow compared to the original, but it is very solid and has a good patina. The screws in it were also too modern (e.g. cross head wood screws) so would need replacing with traditional countersunk slotted head screws.

Door hinges were also forged therefore vary in size, and can easily reach 22" overall. A total of four were required for stable type doors. Modern replacements are often found to have been fitted due to wear and tear of the originals, but it is worth trying to source early wrought iron ones if possible as they look more in keeping. The narrow part of these early hinges that attach to the door frame are invariably 1 1/2" to 2" wide.

Blacksmith forged 'Suffolk style' thumb latches were fitted to Farris doors. The thumb handle assembly which fits on the inside of the door, as well as the flat bar that secures the door on the outside, both normally measure between 7 1/2" to 8 1/2" long. Designs can vary slightly, but a simple and pleasing curve to the interior handle, a weathered appearance (e.g. pitted) and a fairly heavy gauge metal are key factors to look for if ever needing a replacement latch and associated parts. Don't be tempted to fit a cheap modern one, as they look too new, and the flat bar that secures the door shut has a tendency to be too short.

Evidence of a lock and key can sometimes be found on original doors and frames. Examining the outlines of an imprint where an original door

Suffolk latch, hasp, staple & pin.

lock was fitted, the size was 5 1/2" wide x 4 1/4" deep, although this could easily have varied on individual examples. They were positioned just below the interior thumb catch.

A blacksmith made hasp and staple (with additional padlock) was a good alternative as a deterrent to intruders. A Victorian forged hasp pin used to temporary secure a hasp is also an exciting find. Hasp pins found with Farris huts had a fairly wide 'whorl' on the one end, about 1 1/4" wide for easy handling and to prevent it falling through the hasp when in use. The length of the pins were at least 5" long and up to 1/2" thick and were secured to the staple with a small chain.

Stoves

Granaries did not have a stove. They were however, usually included in Farris huts for shepherds, and old tell tale markings on the floor occasionally suggest they were of the cylindrical 'tortoise stove' type (e.g. Charles Portway & Son, Halstead, Essex, number 1 or 2).

Early examples of Portway's stoves had an attractive tortoise cast into their tops, whilst later stoves had a useful lid incorporated into the design for ease of use when topping up logs or coal, and are excellent for boiling a kettle on.

Other English foundries started to produce similar cylindrical type stoves to Charles Portway, thus increasing the likelihood of different makes of stoves of this design sometimes being discovered in huts requiring restoration. Small flat sided stoves and pot bellied stoves are other examples that were also popular to use in shepherds huts and available from other manufacturers. Original stoves are becoming increasingly difficult to find in reasonable condition, so good replacements can command a high price.

Farris hut flues are 3" in diameter, and fitted into the rear or top of a stove (e.g. horizontal or vertical nozzles), and through a cast flue socket that is attached to the outer part of the corrugated roof. The size of original flue sockets are roughly 8 1/4" x 7 1/2" (across the base) with a maximum height of 4", with an internal hole diameter of 3 1/2" for the flue to fit through.

As a guide, Portway number 2 tortoise stoves measure about 2ft high x 1ft wide overall, although other makes can vary slightly. Cast iron trays or stands were also a useful option, with some makes of stoves helping to retain the ash when cleaning them, and providing the floor with additional protection from the heat.

Comparisons of tortoise stoves from a late 1920's catalogue show the most suitable sizes usually found in shepherds' huts.

For example:
Size No.1 (e.g. 20" x 9") gives a heating capacity of 2000 cu. ft.
Size No. 2 (e.g. 24" x 10") gives a heating capacity of 6000 cu. ft.

The heating capacity of a number 2 stove makes it more than adequate for a shepherds hut (size 12 ft x 6 ft). One only has to experience the heat from a stove of this capacity to realise that anything larger would

Tortoise stove advert c.1920's.

C. Portway & Son
Tortoise Stove No. 2 in
a c.1880's J. Farris hut.

SLOW BUT SURE tortoise stove top.

make the interior of a hut uncomfortably hot, and would only increase the potential fire hazard associated with them.

Prices for No.1 and No. 2 tortoise stoves during the late 1920's was between £1 to £1/ 5 shillings, plus extras such as a pan or tray for the floor and installation costs. Market fluctuations would also affect prices.

The interior by the stoves often had galvanised sheeting (e.g. flat or corrugated) surrounding the stove on two sides to protect the wooden panelling from the heat, and flat galvanised sheeting on the floor underneath the stove.

Flat circular shaped sheeting usually surrounded the flue where it went through the ceiling on George Farris huts, whilst John Farris ones normally had flat square shaped sheeting. Stoves were positioned at the rear offside of both brothers' huts as doors were commonly on the nearside. The position of flues in early John Farris huts tend to be positioned slightly closer to the hut

Cast flue socket, flue and cap.

side panelling than George's, allowing room for the stove to fit sideways.

Thomas Hardy's novel *Far from the Madding crowd* gives an exciting account of the dangers of stoves in shepherds' houses as Gabriel Oak was rescued from a fumed filled hut by Bathsheba at the beginning of the story. Certainly, some restoration projects show signs of fire damage caused by carelessness when using stoves, so some form of protection around the stove and good ventilation is advisable. These days, it's also sensible to have a suitable fire extinguisher handy for an emergency.

A No.2 Tortoise stove fitted in a Lott & Walne shepherd's hut. Photo J.L.

Axle Beams & stub axles

The original top front wooden axle beam on Sybil's granary is made up of three sections of timber, which gives the appearance of the underneath being channelled. The three parts bolted together measure 9" in total (4" centre section, 2 1/2" outer sections), and are bolted directly onto the chassis.

J. Farris wrought iron rear axle & stub axles.

This wide top beam configuration is normal on many of George's earlier shepherds' houses and granaries, and can often be found on derelict examples (e.g. with the large rectangular name plate) requiring restoration.

The lower front beam on Sybil's granary may have been replaced during its lifetime, but matched the original design associated with these axles.

An additional piece of timber is positioned centrally on the top of the lower axle beam, and the bottom part of the turntable is bolted directly onto it, with two special bolts. These are 10 3/4" long x 1/2" thick, with a 1 1/4" wide flattened bolt head that lies flush within the countersunk hole in the turntable casting. A washer and square nut are used to secure it to the beam. The timber is therefore sandwiched in between the axle and turntable.

The existing piece of wood was still sound so it was treated with a preservative and reused. This consists of a block of wood, 37 1/2" long, tapering down to 26 1/2", resembling a wedge shape at each end. The longest end is positioned on the top of the lower axle beam. The turntable is located on top of the narrower section. The width of the block (or spacer) is 5 3/8" x 3" thick, but may vary on other huts.

It's worth noting that the lower axle beam ends protrude over the stub axle blocks by 1 3/4". This also applies to the rear axle beam. It appears that these protruding ends were included to prevent rain dripping off the roof directly onto the stub axle assembly.

The granaries rear axle was cut as a single beam, with wooden spacers used between the individual chassis members and axle. These spacers are necessary to help provide the correct distance and overall height between the chassis and axle, thereby ensuring the hut is level.

Granary

Top front axle beam. 73" x 9" x 4" deep
  (three parts bolted together = 9").
Lower front axle beam. 72" x 6" x 6".
Wooden block on lower beam that turntable is bolted onto.
  37 1/2" long (attaches to lower axle beam).
  26 1/2" long (turntable positioned on top).
  Width is 5 3/8. Thickness is 3".
Rear axle beam. 72" x 6" x 6".
Rear axle to chassis wooden spacers (x 4). 3 3/4" deep.

G. Farris wooden axle & J. Farris iron axle with different designs of turntables.

The granary axles are made from softwood which is quite usual on Farris huts. As previously mentioned, hardwoods such as Oak were not as popular as one would expect. Some Farris restorations provide evidence of original softwood axles on the rear, with front axles having been replaced in a hardwood.

Front and rear wooden axle beams seem to generally be standard on most George Farris huts. However, examination of early John Farris shepherds' houses suggests that some appeared to have had wooden front axles (top and lower beams) and sometimes wooden or wrought iron square section rear axles. A wooden top beam and wrought iron bottom front axle, and iron rear axle (approx. 1 1/2" to 2" thick), became a popular option, making iron axles a distinguishing feature of John Farris huts.

Investigation of a later example by John Farris & Sons (e.g. small rectangular name plate) was found to have a wooden front and rear axle, although the lower front axle beam and rear axle had apparently been renewed at some time.

Smaller Farris huts, such as the granary, tend to have their top front wooden axle beams bolted directly to the chassis. This appears consistent with both George and John's smaller huts. Sometimes these beams are referred to as front cross members.

George's larger shepherds' houses have a wooden spacer block inserted between the chassis and front top beam. These are about 1 3/4" deep. Rear wooden axle beams were attached with larger wooden blocks, around 4" deep, located between the axle and the four main individual chassis members.

John Farris (& Sons) large shepherds' houses had deeper wooden blocks (approx. 3" high) between the top front wooden axle beam and chassis members, on both their wooden and iron front axles designs. Their chassis' also differed as they commonly had five long beams (e.g. 3" wide x 5" deep) running the length of their huts. The front of the central chassis beam did not have a wooden spacer block due to the turntable pin positioning. Huts with wooden rear axles had deeper blocks between axle and chassis, but this did not apply to ones with wrought iron rear axles.

A number of George's larger and later shepherds' huts that I have examined appear to have a solid wooden top beam with narrow spacers sandwiched between the beam and chassis. It is possible that this solid beam was a modification made by the foundry. Many axles have been replaced over the years, so there is a 'grey area' with the evidence that I have researched, but the consistency of later models with this design does suggest that a solid top beam could also have originally been included on George's huts.

Certainly, my research suggests that John Farris (& Sons) wooden top beams were made in one piece, which included deeper wooden spacers between the beam and chassis on their larger models.

An example of a J. Farris shepherd's hut researched had a top front wooden beam measuring 70 1/2" x 6" x 6" deep (with a spacer block 3" high), and lower wooden axle beam 74" x 6" x 6". The top axle beam tapered down to 4" deep on the ends.

The thickness and length of timber axles does appear to vary a little between Farris huts measured, so it is perhaps prudent to make an exact copy of the original one fitted, if it appears correct. Exceptions and slight variations will always exist, partly due to modifications carried out during the huts construction, and because they are individually hand built.

I have studied another of George's huts with an early name plate with a steel front axle and rear wooden one. It had the wrong wheels, so may have been altered during its life time. However, the rest of it was typical of George's usual design, including small window, door at the rear, narrow wooden curved roof support beam, and horizontal beam that runs around the interior panelling.

John Farris rear wrought iron axles were usually attached with sturdy 'V' shaped wrought iron support brackets, about 1ft deep. They were secured to the near side and offside of the chassis with robust bolts, and to the axle with heavy duty forged 'U' bolts. There was not usually a 'V' shaped support bracket attached to the centre of the rear of the chassis and centre of the rear iron axle on early models, although I have seen one fitted on a later example. This modification was certainly included by some competitors to help strengthen the rear axle beam (e.g. prevent it from bending) and increase support to the rear floor section. John Farris also made heavy duty axle castings for use on some elevators. This type of casting has been discovered under a couple of unrestored shepherds' huts (in-between the chassis and rear axle), and in one case, used to sling the wheels underneath the body. The name plates were missing, but similarities in overall design makes this an intriguing area requiring further investigation.

Enough about the axle beams. It's now time to elaborate about the stub axles!

George Farris front and rear wrought iron stub axles can be between 23 1/2" to 25" in total (including wheel, cap, casting and axle mounting sections), and are commonly individually tapered to fit the Farris spoked wheels.

Once in a while, stub axles and wheels might be found without any obvious taper, although this is usually more of an exception rather than the rule.

The granary stub axles measure 23 1/2" long overall and are 1 3/4" thick, tapering down to 1 1/2" on the wheel and cap end, which also has a 1/2" punched hole for a large 5" long split pin. The opposite end that is secured to the wooden axle is flattened for about 2 1/2" with a 3/4" punched hole for the axle bolt.

Granary stub axle. Cracks can occur where they are bolted to the axle beam.

Left: Rear stub axle, block & brace.
Right: Front stub axle & cast iron block.

George's stub axles are located into cast iron stub axle blocks that are attached to the timber axles. All four blocks are individually recessed into the axle ends.

The granary blocks measure 6" long x 2 3/4" wide x 3 1/4" deep. An additional 7/8" thick plate, positioned underneath to secure each stub axle in place, gives an overall depth of 4 1/4". The granary rear blocks are 1/4" longer than the front ones, and measure 6 1/4". The plates are the same thickness as the front ones, but they are 9 1/4" long, allowing for a 'lip' to bolt the side rear braces onto. Two bolts per axle block, up to 9 1/2" x 3/8" thick with appropriate washers and square nuts holds the whole assembly together.

Slight variations do exist. A later George Farris shepherd's house (e.g. oblong name plate) had blocks measuring 6" long x 2 3/4" wide x 2 3/4" deep, front and rear. It also had thinner 1/2" plates giving a depth of 3 1/4" overall. The rear plates were also longer than the front ones as they included a lip used to attach the side braces, which are explained in more detail shortly.

John Farris stub axle castings fitted onto wooden axles are different to George's axle blocks. Example measured were approximately 6" long x 2 1/2" wide where they are positioned underneath the axle. The front and rear of the casting is right angled and locates either side of the axle beam by about 3", curving down centrally by roughly 1" around the stub axle, therefore does not have an additional plate bolted underneath as with George's design. The depth of the casting including the central curve to hold the stub axle in place is in the region of 5" overall. Two 8 1/2" bolts and square nuts holds each casting in place.

Stub axle lengths on John's huts are about 28 1/2" in total, including wheel, cap, casting and axle mounting section.

John Farris shepherds' houses with iron front and rear axles, including the stub axles, would have been forged by them and made in one piece in wrought iron. Axle beams measure approximately 74" long in-between the stub axles.

The use of wrought iron and cast iron was common on shepherd's huts, but can sometimes be a little confusing when trying to distinguish between them.

Wrought iron was an excellent old fashion iron alloy material, produced by puddling pig iron while molten, and was ideal for making items such as nails, bolts and axles, for shepherds' huts. It was fibrous and tough, and had a low carbon content, and was easy to work by the blacksmith, as it was soft and malleable. True wrought iron ceased in the 1970's. Many products described as wrought iron these days are actually mild steel.

Cast iron on the other hand, is hard and brittle as it has a higher carbon content than wrought iron. It is a ferrous alloy (usually made from pig iron) that is heated until it liquefies and then poured into moulds and allowed to cool and harden into the desired shape. This process was used to produce castings such as Farris wheels and stub axle blocks.

Rear axle support braces

This is a useful section to explain about braces. These were used on a shepherd's hut to give additional strength and support to various parts of its construction. Axles often require extra support to help spread the load when the hut is being towed, and braces are added for this purpose.

If one examines either side of the rear axles on George's huts (behind the rear wheels) it becomes evident that the two stub axle blocks have a flat wrought iron brace bolted to a 'lip' incorporated into the casting design. This leads forward from the stub axle area to the chassis frame (on both sides) to provide additional support and stability thereby helping to take the strain from the front axle when the hut is being towed.

Granary rear axle support brace.

Where the brace is bolted to the casting, the lip has a tendency to fracture after years of abuse, and modifications such as repairs or replacement may be apparent.

The size of the brace is normally 26 1/2" x 1 1/2" x 3/8" thick. The coach bolt that attaches the brace to the side of the chassis ideally needs to be about 5 1/2" long x 1/2" thick on George's huts. This takes into account the depth of the chassis (e.g. 4"), thickness of the brace, washer and nut.

Removal of the iron brace where it attaches to the chassis usually ends with the nut either shearing or requiring grinding off if badly corroded onto the bolt. This can be a real nuisance, as it is necessary to remove some of the floorboards in order to extract the remains of the concealed coach bolt that had been inserted through a hole in the top of the chassis, before the boards were hammered in place.

There are instances where the floorboards have been drilled in order to extract and replace these offending bolts. Not an ideal situation, but an understandable one when considering the work involved when a replacement is necessary.

The correct method is to remove the boards carefully without damaging them (or the chassis), which is not an easy task due to them having been nailed in place for years. This is always challenging and time consuming, but is my preferred option, and unfortunately has been necessary with the granary. The reward is good detailing and the opportunity to investigate any other potential problems that could eventually arise in this area of the chassis at a later date, whilst the floorboards have been removed.

The head of the coach bolt is sunken into the wooden chassis to allow for the floorboards to fit flush. Check for age related cracks or damage in this area. It may be necessary to include a strengthening steel plate between the head of the bolt and the top of a chassis if cracks have developed in the timber. A plate, 8" x 1 1/2" x 1/8"

thick will suffice. A 5/8" hole drilled in the middle of the plate will be adequate to accept a 1/2" thick bolt. Similar plates may also be useful in other locations of a chassis where cracks are evident.

The underneath of the floorboards can always be modified slightly in order to compensate for any unevenness that may occur due to the addition of a strengthening plate.

Trying to find replacement coach bolts can also be problematic. Although plated metric bolts may be available 'off the shelf', it is far preferable to try and source old imperial stock that will look correct and blend with existing ironwork and fixings.

Detailing of a rear axle support brace.

Interestingly, one of George's oval name plate shepherds' houses previously examined had a forged 3/4" wrought iron rear axle support bar, 37" long (including where it bolts onto the stub axle casting and chassis) that appeared so well made, it could easily have been an original part. I have also found similar braces on a couple of other later huts, but it is uncertain if these were original or replacements parts.

John Farris huts with rear wrought iron axles lacked iron side support braces, but I've come across rounded bars (or braces) included on a J. Farris & Sons example (e.g. small rectangular name plate) with a rear wooden axle.

Two other huts examined (without name plates) also had iron braces, and were attached through the wooden rear axle. One hut (e.g. 12ft x 6ft) had 3/4" thick wrought iron bars that were 42" long. The length was 6 1/2" where they were secured and bolted through the axle with a large washer and nut, and 35 1/2" long where they continued up and were attached to the underneath of the outer chassis members. The ends had a familiar 'arrow head' which is quite usual on John's ironwork. A single bolt on each side went through the floorboards and chassis and a square nut was tightened from underneath to hold them in place.

My research is suggesting that some of John's huts may have had side braces on their wooden rear axles, but further investigation is necessary with examples that have original name plates attached, in order to clarify my observations more clearly.

G. Farris detail of front axle & turntable. Photo J.L.

Turntables

The turntable fitted to Farris wooden front axles is a robust cast iron two piece circular type plate (with rectangular ends or 'lugs' that rest on the beams) with a long wrought iron pin through it, and allows for easy turning of the smaller front wheels to pass under the front of the chassis when cornering. Turntables usually measure about 19" (including the lugs) by 15 1/2", although sizes may vary slightly on some huts. The thickness of each casting is 7/8", making a maximum depth of 1 3/4" when the two turntable plates are put together.

   The iron pin on the granary measures 17 1/2" long and 1 1/4" diameter. The pin is peened over on one end (approx. 2" across) and it has a 1" slot the opposite end where a flat 3" long x 3/8" thick 'L' shaped cotter pin (or wedge), washer and split pin are used to secure it. The iron pin is pushed upwards through the assembled bottom axle beam, turntable and top beam and secured at the top. Pins do vary in size, with an example on a larger Farris hut (e.g. oblong name plate) measuring 18 1/2" long x 1 1/2" diameter.

A rare front axle turntable stating 'Farris Maker Coombe Bissett'.

The granary turntable plate is unusually secured to the top beam with four
6" x 1/2" thick countersunk bolts (including washers and square nuts), and two
longer bolts, washers and nuts for the lower beam, as previously mentioned.
Farris turntable plates normally have two bolts top and bottom. The granary
turntable is 15 1/4" at its narrowest width, and 18 3/4" including its side lugs that
rest on the axle beam. The central hole for the pin is 1 1/2" wide.

Some of the George Farris turntables had 'Farris, Maker, Coombe, Salisbury'
included on the top casting and are quite rare.

Turntables on John Farris wrought iron front axles differ. The lower half of the
turntable is bolted onto a wide iron 'A' frame that is attached above the iron axle
with 'U' bolts, whilst the top half of the turntable is positioned against the
underside of the wooden beam that is secured underneath the front of the chassis.
A long iron pin goes through the whole assembly (e.g. iron axle, through the
turntable and wooden top beam). The cast iron turntable has no 'end lugs',
but is recognisable with a raised 'lip' on the top casting which the wooden beam
rests against.

Wrought iron turntable pin.

J. Farris iron axle layout (horseshoe name plate)
with a central axle support bar.

Front axle support bar,
brake chains & drag shoes

Smaller George Farris huts, such as their granaries, appear not to have had a
wrought iron central axle support bar (or brace) used to help spread the load of the
axle when being towed by a horse. This rounded bar was usually included on many
of George's larger shepherds' houses, although I have noted an early large George
Farris example with original front axle fitted, and the same name badge as Sybil's
hut, which showed no evidence of having one. Research of a couple of George's
shepherds' houses (e.g. oval name plate) were also found to be lacking this bar.

Support bars measure about 60" long x 1 1/4" thick on George's huts and are
attached to the bottom of the large pin that runs through the front axle turntable
plate, and back towards a central wooden chassis mounting support. This consists
of a piece of timber, 32" x 4" x 2 3/4" deep, which is secured by two 9" x 1/2" thick
bolts that go through holes drilled in the two central chassis beams (before the
floorboards are hammered down) and subsequently holds the timber in place with
the use of washers and square nuts. The timber itself may be nicely rounded on the
ends close to where it is bolted onto the chassis.

The support bar at the axle end has a large circular forged 'eye' which the pin
goes through to secure it to the front axle assembly. The end located onto the
central chassis mounting, resembles a 'U' section that is bolted onto a 1" wide

forged bolt with appropriate eye that is located vertically through the centre of the timber that is attached to the two inner chassis members. The width of the exterior of the 'U' section is 2 1/2" wide, the internal measurement is 1 1/4". The central bolt with eye is about 6" long.

Sometimes, modifications have been carried out during a restoration which have resulted in a completely different style of axle support bar or brace made and fitted.

A couple of examples of John's earlier large huts with wooden front axles (e.g. circular name plates) that have been researched, had no evidence of an iron bar ever being bolted to the centre of the chassis. Interestingly, two very early derelict shepherds' houses, thought to possibly be made by John Farris, but missing their name plates, showed remains of their wooden front axles with no evidence of a central support bar ever being fitted either.

However, John's shepherds' houses that had a wooden top beam and bottom wrought iron front axle (either circular or horseshoe name plates) did have a bar fitted. Not to have included one would have resulted in too much load being put on the wrought iron axle and the bolts securing it. These were attached to the bottom of the turntable pin and bolted directly onto the central chassis beam.

Inspecting an example by John Farris & Sons, with wooden front and rear axles, showed that it also had a central axle support bar that appeared original, thereby indicating that front axle support bars were probably included on some of the later Shaftesbury made huts with wooden axles.

No doubt more idiosyncrasies will emerge with new discoveries of both George's and John's huts, but care has to be taken not to draw inaccurate conclusions from examining examples that may have been altered or modified over the years.

Some hut makers also adopted the use of a chain instead of an iron bar for this purpose on their wooden axles. I have noticed examples of chains (or iron bars) being attached from the front axle assembly all the way back to the rear axle, rather than a central chassis location as with Farris models.

John Farris shepherds' houses also had a wrought iron 'support brace' located under each side of the front top timber axle beam, which was also attached to the side wooden chassis frame. George's didn't have these front side braces. Supports were about 3/4" thick x 2ft long, and the ends flattened and shaped in the forge to locate under the top beam where they were secured with the two bolts and nuts that hold the beam into place. The end attached to the chassis is fastened with one bolt and nut.

The chassis frames also provided a location for 'brake chain' brackets, which appear to be more common on John's huts than George's, and can usually be found on the nearside chassis beam in between the front and rear wheels.

Brake chain brackets on John's huts, situated nearer the front wheel were 9" long (6" curving down to a lower 3" section), 1 1/2" wide and 1/4" thick. Attached to this bracket was another one which was 7 1/2" long and was linked to a robust chain measuring close to 60" in length. A rather clever linkage was also incorporated into the design, in order to quickly attach and secure the chain around the rear wheel. An additional bracket located into the side of the chassis, nearer the rear wheel,

John Farris Hut (circular name plate) showing front top axle beam with chassis side support irons, cast iron turntable, brake chain and drag shoe.

was also included on early J. Farris shepherds' houses and ran downwards from the chassis 3 3/4" and then curved back on itself 3" with a forged arrow end. This was useful for holding chains and drag shoes.

There are no rear brake chain (or drag shoe) brackets on Sybil's granary. Brake chains were often used on horse drawn huts by attaching a chain usually around a rear wheel through its spokes and securing it to a brake chain bracket positioned on the chassis, thereby locking the wheel and preventing it from turning. Although a very crude method of braking, it was effective, and can be found on other agricultural carts of the same period.

Farris wheels, especially on the larger and heavier models, often show signs of stress, such as bent spokes, chips and fractures, which would have partly been due to the stresses of the brake chain, as well as the rough surfaces they would have had to travel over. Luckily, wheels could (and still can) be repaired by a blacksmith who is able to shrink and attach a traditional iron band repair around the wheel to hold everything together.

Modern welding methods of wheels is another alternative, but research and recommendation of good specialists needs to be adhered to, in order to ensure successful results can be guaranteed when repairing old castings.

It's astonishing the rough treatment that some wheels have had to endure during their years of service and are still useable, albeit with a little repair and attention. It is not uncommon to find wheels that have had iron bands added years ago, with old band repairs showing obvious signs of flat spots where the wheel has been 'skidded' due to the regular use of a brake chain.

Luckily, Sybil's granary wheels overall appear to be in remarkably good condition (although seized solid) as it probably had less abuse over the years when compared to the harsh conditions that some heavier shepherds' houses had to endure.

A cast iron drag shoe with chain (also referred to as a drug shoe, chock, slipper, wedge or skid), was another accessory and useful item for all sizes of huts and carts, where it could be wedged under a wheel to 'lock it' into position, acting as another crude form of braking on slopes, or securing the hut when stationery. When finding and purchasing an original drag shoe, it's important to check the internal width of it, as shoes do vary in size. A minimum internal width of 4 1/2" is required for Farris rear wheels. Interestingly, John Farris (& Sons) cast and sold their own drag shoes over the years in various sizes, and were clearly marked with their name and size on each individual casting.

Farris Wheels

When one admires a shepherd's hut or granary, the wheels can be one of the most important and attractive features of the whole construction. Original Farris spoked wheels do not disappoint!

Traditional Farris wheels are very distinguishable as they are large and heavy duty and have a cast iron hub (e.g. middle section), a cast iron rim (e.g. outer section), and wrought iron spokes, 5/8" thick. Many competitors wheels were just cast iron.

Sybil recalls Farris wheels being cast at the Coombe Bissett foundry whilst she was a child, and refers to how they were made in her 'Foreword' at the beginning of this book. She also commented that 'Uncle Jim attended, and carried a cauldron of molten iron which he poured into black moulds for the wheels'.

Sybil's granary has 26" eight spoke front wheels, and 35 3/4" ten spoke rear cast iron wheels, positioned on the outside of the bodywork, with its original stub axle caps fitted. Front wheels used on Farris shepherds' houses were usually about 25" high, with 35" to 36" (referred to as 3ft) wheels on the rear. The width of the rims on the larger rear wheels are also slightly wider than on the smaller front wheels.

Certainly, moderate shrinkage of the wheel castings during their manufacture is a factor to consider when measuring and comparing wheels, and it's not that unusual to find slight variations with individual wheel sizes when measured accurately.

A set of early Farris wheels.

Farris stub axle end cap with slots.

Stub axle end caps usually have a couple of slots on the outer edge where a blacksmith made cotter pin is inserted through in order to secure a cap to a stub axle. A large split pin can be attached to the bottom of the cotter pin to prevent it falling out. Sometimes, caps with simple round holes to accept a large split pin, rather than a cotter pin, can be found. The granary caps consist of 5/8" round drilled holes.

The diameter of the granary stub axle end caps measure approximately 3 3/4" wide where they rest against the wheel hub, and 2 1/4" wide where its secured by a split pin. The depth is 2". However, the external sizes of some other Farris caps measured were slightly smaller, so variations can be expected.

There appears to also be a couple of different internal sizes for Farris caps, depending on the stub axles

Granary stub axle end cap.

Front wheels with ten spokes, occasionally found on some later Farris huts.

thickness. Recast or replacement caps need to be selected for their suitability and ideally machined to fit individual stub axles accurately.

Farris wheel hubs and stub axles are normally slightly tapered, being bespoke to fit individual components. As previously discussed, tapering of stub axles can easily vary from around 1 3/4" down to about 1 1/2" (on the cap end), making it difficult to match a replacement wheel with an existing original stub axle.

Early George Farris and John Farris huts usually had front wheels with eight spokes and rear wheels with ten spokes. However, observation of a John Farris & Sons, and some later George Farris examples have been discovered with ten spokes on the front and rear wheels, leading to speculation that the design of the front wheels may have been altered in later years. More about this later!

The circumference of the front wheel hubs also appear slightly narrower on the ten spoked wheels examined, but were still tapered internally to fit the Farris stub axles. Front hubs with eight spokes are overall larger and bulkier, similar to the rear wheel design on all models. The depth of the granary wheel hubs are 6 7/8" (plus stub axle end caps which are approx. 2" deep). Ten spoke front wheel hubs can measure up to 7 1/4" deep. Tapered shafts can vary between 9" to 10" long. All Farris spoked wheels have a protruding cast 'lug' on the outer ends of individual spokes that are located under the inner raised edge of the wheel rim, and on the outer edge of the wheel hub.

The following details show subtle differences in size between the granaries eight spoke front wheels and the ten spoke front wheels that I have seen and measured on some George Farris later huts.

Granary front wheels.

Height of wheel.	26"
Width of rim.	3 7/8"
Number of spokes.	8
Thickness of spokes.	5/8"
Length of spokes.	8 1/2" (between inner & outer rims)
Hub thickness.	5" (between spokes)
Hub depth.	6 7/8"
Tapered hub fit (approx.)	2 1/4" tapering down to 1 1/2"

Granary rear wheels.

Height of wheel.	35 3/4"
Width of rim.	4"
Number of spokes.	10
Thickness of spokes.	5/8"
Length of spokes.	12 7/8" (between inner & outer rims)
Hub thickness.	5 1/4" (between spokes)
Hub depth.	6 7/8"
Tapered hub fit (approx.)	2 1/4" tapering down to 1 1/2"

Farris shepherd's hut.

Front wheels (e.g. discovered on some later huts).

Height of wheel.	24 1/2"
Width of rim.	3 3/4"
Number of spokes.	10
Thickness of spokes.	5/8"
Length of spokes.	8 1/4" (between inner & outer rims)
Hub thickness.	3 1/4" at ends (4 1/2" between spokes)
Hub depth.	7 1/4"
Tapered hub fit (approx.)	1 3/4" tapering down to 1 1/2"

Rear wheels (e.g. oblong name plate).

Height of wheel.	35 1/2"
Width of rim.	4"
Number of spokes.	10
Thickness of spokes.	5/8"
Length of spokes.	12 7/8" (between inner & outer rims)
Hub thickness.	5" (between spokes)
Hub depth.	7 1/4"
Tapered hub fit (approx.)	1 3/4" tapering down to 1 1/2"

Nb. Further reference to the number of spokes in Farris wheels is discussed under the heading George Farris name plates.

Farris wheels often incorporate a small pipe (or tube) in the hubs to enable oiling of the stub axles and wheels. A 'stopper' made from cork could be used to seal the ends. Thick 'steam oil' would have been ideal as a lubrication.

A good application of grease is recommended when reassembling wheels onto their stub axles during a restoration, unless of course one happens to have some extremely thick steam oil at hand!

Genuine spoked wheels that were fitted to George Farris and John Farris shepherds' houses and granaries are increasingly becoming difficult to find and subsequently command a high price if needing replacing. Certainly, examples that are found on huts requiring restoration often have signs of fractures, chips and bent spokes, but the cost of repairing them can still be cheaper and easier than sourcing original or alternative replacements. However, it is certainly worth studying and measuring original wheels if looking for replacements, as there are similar but incorrect spoked wheels that were used by other businesses on their own shepherds' huts, carts and agricultural machinery, including some elevators.

For example, caution should be taken of similar ten spoke front wheels, which are just under 24" tall with slightly less bulky hubs, as they may have straight and smaller diameter non tapered internals to fit onto a stub axle. Wheels with oversized non tapered internal hub diameters are also a problem as they are not compatible with the tapered Farris stub axles. It is easy to be caught out, as I have found from experience!

Large rear wheels are even harder to find, with other companies variations sometimes based on a similar design to Farris wheels, but usually found to be of a slightly different size overall. Extra spokes and subtle differences to the casting can all add to the confusion (and frustration) when trying to match damaged existing Farris wheels during a restoration project. Such wheels, however, may prove in some circumstances to be a very good substitute if supplied with their original stub axles, or found to fit reasonably well on to the existing Farris stub axles without major modification necessary, due to the difficulty in finding original examples.

One of the problems in finding replacement wheels for many shepherds' houses, is that dealers and enthusiasts over the last few years have bought old original wheels to use on reproduction huts, as this can sometimes prove more cost effective than having new ones cast, and certainly provides an authentic selling point to their customers. This subsequently increases the prices of the good and rarer examples, such as the spoked wheels fitted to both George and John Farris huts.

Inevitably, there will always be a few derelict restoration projects discovered without their wheels attached. This could be due to a number of reasons, but the increase in demand and value of original wheels increases the likelihood of a few unscrupulous people removing them from historic huts without permission of the owner. The attempted theft of Sybil's granary is a timely reminder to ensure both huts and wheels are secure against theft.

Granary front axle beam, turntable & horse shafts.

Horse shafts

Sybil's portable granary has evidence that it used to have wooden horse shafts, designed for a single horse, as there is a blacksmith made wrought iron securing hook attached to the front nearside corrugated panel, used to secure the shafts horizontally when not in use. This is quite common on earlier Farris huts where a horse was used to move it. A description of these horse shaft hooks has previously been discussed and compared with the door hooks.

Later examples would have been towed by tractor, which were becoming popular in Britain during the 1920's, and may possibly be found with a hook central top, nearer the wooden roof apex end board, as an iron 'A' frame tow bar would have been used and secured in an upright position accordingly. Many early shepherds' houses, however, have been modified over the years and fitted with iron tow bars but still retain their original shaft hook.

George Farris huts had a forged iron hook attached to an 'eye' on a thickish thread with bolt situated on the nearside front panel. John Farris models usually

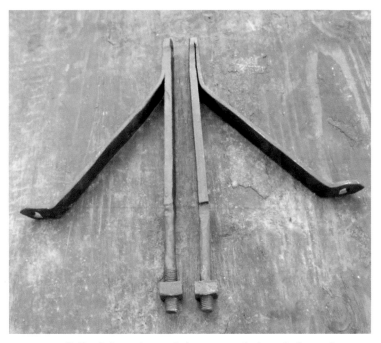

G. Farris lower front axle beam wrought iron shaft attachments.

used a round 'staple' type securing 'eye' attached through the corrugated sheeting and frame to secure a forged hook to the nearside front panel, or sometimes a chain and hook located on the offside sheet. The height where hooks were located also varied.

Evidence of hooks, when missing, can usually be found on the front corrugation due to a hole, dents or grooves caused from their use over the years. The latter can give a good indication of their actual size.

All Farris horse shafts were very long and curved near the opening end. They were usually made from hardwood such as seasoned ash, which provided a strong timber that was easy to bend and resistant to splitting, although any suitable timber could have been used, depending on availability and cost. When shafts were not in use they could be hinged back into an upward position against the front of the bodywork and secured in place with the securing hook or chain. When in this erect position, the shafts would protrude above the height of the roof. Original front roof sheets often show signs of where the shafts have bashed against them.

One of the reasons horse shafts were so long on shepherds' houses, compared to other wheeled carriages, is that the shafts were positioned fairly low on the front axle, and the extra length was required to give enough distance from the hut for the horse when towing was necessary.

The wooden shafts on Farris huts were also designed with a 'wooden ladder' incorporated into its rear section to add strength and durability due to its long length. Blacksmith made ironwork was also incorporated into the design to add strength to the shafts and to

Farris wooden horse shafts.

J. Farris hut with shafts.

provide the necessary hooks for the horse tackle to be secured adequately.

Farris huts had two wrought iron 'eyes' bolted to the ladder end of the wooden horse shafts. These line up adjacent to the holes in the wrought iron shaft attachments on the front axle lower beam. Both are held in place with a round bar (or pin) usually about 42" long x 3/4" thick, which allows for the shafts to pivot upwards to be secured by the hook situated on the bodywork.

Evidence from one of Sybil's old photographs does show that some later John Farris & Sons shepherds' houses had forged 'eyes' bolted to the horse shafts, but included a curve in the wrought ironwork which would have increased the height of the shafts slightly.

Finding original shafts is increasingly unlikely, although old wooden shafts similar to the Farris design can provide some useful hooks, brackets and chains if contemplating making new ones. Farris shafts are believed to have measured in the region of 115" long x 40" across the width of the ladder.

Romantic retreat.

Romantic Retreat

An ancient piece of history,
Seduction from the past,
Surrounded in mystery,
It's love at first sight.

The wonders of ageing,
More beautiful with time,
Makes life worth engaging,
No conflict, no strife.

Perfect with imperfections,
Battered and torn,
With beautiful reflections,
By the calm, still waters.

Admirers in the sunlight,
A twinkle in the eye,
A lover's ambitious fight
To slow changing and decay.

A pose that is so elegant,
Standing tall and proud,
Everything seems irrelevant.
Such an astonishing sight!

The daytime is for living,
Night time is to love,
Life should be for giving,
A romantic retreat.

Rollin

Restoration of Sybil's portable granary

A certain amount of preservation and restoration work had been carried out on Sybil's granary over the year's whilst back at the Coombe Bissett site. Replacement steps, door, and the wooden roof apex end boards, just below the roof line, had been replaced. The renewal of the door and end boards were necessary to keep the hut weather proof, and the majority of the original floor has subsequently survived.

It was decided to complete some more restoration work whilst at Bere Regis, where the granary would benefit from some professional help with the axles, rear chassis member and un-seizing of the wheels.

Inspecting the Wheels.

The granary and wheels had been painted to help with its preservation. Although some Farris wheels are sometimes found to be painted red, un-restored huts and restoration projects can occasionally show signs of remnants of blue paint on their wheels. More about this later!

The seized wheels needed to be regularly soaked with diesel for over four months in order to free them. It was decided not to use a press to free the wheels from the stub axles as this method is fraught with dangers for old castings, and would also have required the removal of the original wheel caps which could have become damaged.

Sometimes wheels are put onto open fires to free them from the stub axles, but this can also be quite precarious and perhaps a little unwise due to the danger of heat causing fractures to the wheel castings. If this occurs, a competent blacksmith should be able to apply a steel ring to the wheels to hold them together.

Once freed, the wheels were checked, and one was found to be slightly buckled and ran 'untrue' thereby having a slight wobble. I think if I was around 100 years old, I would probably feel the same! This however, was quite acceptable as long as it didn't foul the bodywork, and may have been caused during the attempted theft of the granary.

Inspecting the axles

The wooden front axle beams looked fairly sound, but on closer inspection needed replacing due to the axle ends being rotten. An exact copy was made. The axle ends are often a problem as water runs off the roof and drips onto the wooden axle beam, and in time causes decay. A traditional solution was to put some lead over the beam ends to protect them from the dripping water. Some restorers reduce the width of the axles by a few inches to help avoid this problem but one has to be careful that the wheels don't fowl the side of the bodywork.

During the restoration process it was planned to use a steam engine to turn a vintage saw bench in order to cut new front axle beams for the granary. A large tree trunk would be placed onto a vintage saw and cut to size, being powered by steam, reminiscent of how the timber would have been cut during the Victorian and Edwardian periods. For anyone vaguely interested in steam, it's certainly worth reading on!

It is also necessary when replacing the axles to change the long axle securing bolts, as these over time become wafer thin and will probably shear off when attempting to undo them. Removal of some of the floorboards to replace the original axle bolts will be necessary on George Farris huts. It is important to replace the axle bolts, square nuts and floorboard nails with hand made blacksmith copies to retain correct detailing and authenticity.

George Farris designed his huts with bolts securing the axles being hidden under the floorboards. John Farris huts were made with the floor nailed in place, and then the bolts went through the floorboards to secure the axles, leaving the head of the bolt on show.

It's not uncommon to find George Farris huts that have

Eddie Butterfield cutting a new Farris front axle beam.

The 1918 Stenner & Gunn No.4 rack saw bench in action.

had replacement axles to have been fitted with modern type threads and bolts drilled and inserted directly through the floorboards, rather than correct forged bolts being used and located under the floorboards to the original specification

Sizes and quantities of bolts could be quite variable. For example, it was found that during a restoration of an early John Farris hut, the forged chassis to front axle bolts were up to 14" long, 9" long for stub axles secured onto the bottom wooden beam, and about 7" long to secure 'U' brackets for the wrought iron rear axle.

Bolts are 1/2" thick, of varying lengths, with a BSW (British Standard Whitworth) thread and appropriate square forged nut. A total of eighteen bolts of similar size may be required for some J. Farris examples that have iron rear axles and brackets for brake chains, etc. However, variations in bolt lengths and quantities are to be expected between the two brothers huts due to the thickness of their chassis', floorboards, axles and relevant brackets that may secure them.

Fortunately, the original wooden rear axle on Sybil's granary was still in reasonable condition and hadn't been modernised in any way. The ends would require some attention as there were signs of cracking, and the sheared bolts that secured the stub axles to the wooden beam needed renewing.

The bolts securing the axle to the chassis had also become wafer thin over the years, and were replaced whilst the rear floorboards had been removed. At the same time, four replacement wooden spacer blocks (e.g. 3 3/4" deep), were positioned between the individual chassis beams and rear axle to ensure strength and rigidity in this region. Due to the size and weight of a hut, it may be advisable, if only for health and safety reasons, to consider asking a specialist to replace or repair

A new blacksmith made chassis to axle bolt being forged.
Note the shortened remains of the original corroded Farris bolt.

*French Marshall Britannia
Steam engine c.1910.*

85

axles and chassis timbers that may require lifting facilities or specialist equipment and tools. With a sound rolling chassis, which is essential, all the other jobs should be fairly manageable for a competent and practical enthusiast, which will help keep the overall restoration costs down.

If choosing this option, it is obviously necessary to do your research and select a recommended professional specialist that can give correct advice and a reasonable estimate, and is capable and trustworthy of carrying out accurate work where conservation and authenticity is a priority. Alternatively, if you have the expertise, facilities and time to complete a full restoration yourself, you should find it a rewarding and enjoyable experience.

Inspecting the chassis

It is also very important to inspect underneath a shepherd's house or granary to check the condition of the wooden chassis. The rear chassis beam and the rear of the side chassis timbers are very prone to rot and decay if water has entered the hut through an ill fitted door (or lack of door) or hole in the roof where a flue and stove has been removed. If the rear floor looks in very poor condition, damage to these chassis beams is likely. Sometimes, the chassis can be braced where minor rot or damage is evident, but it is crucial to use blacksmith made ironwork to ensure the bracing looks authentic and in keeping with the overall era.

If more severe damage to the chassis has occurred then it's going to be a more challenging and costly restoration project. It is very difficult to replace the outer chassis side beams on shepherds' houses without removal of the body as the wooden floor, interior wooden panelling and exterior corrugated sheeting are built against these chassis beams, therefore really requiring professional help, experience and lifting equipment to replace or repair the timbers properly.

Fortunately, apart from some serious decay to the rear beam just underneath the rear floorboards, near the door entrance, the chassis on Sybil's granary was overall in fairly sound condition for its age. There were a few splits in the chassis (especially where the floorboards had been nailed into position) and a couple of areas near the rear end that were far from perfect, but one can hardly expect perfection with timber of such an age. The rear chassis beam therefore needed to be replaced and a wood treatment applied generously in order to help preserve it and prevent further rot.

It is always a concern when replacing the rear chassis beam. A lot depends on whether the original stub tenon joints and mortise and tenon joints are still in reasonable condition and will prise apart successfully to allow a replacement section to be installed. If not, more drastic and expensive action may be required. Sometimes it is possible to cut out any rot and glue and clamp a piece of new wood into place, or even attach a forged iron bracket to add additional support and strength. All options concerning the chassis are time consuming and difficult to achieve successfully, and

Rot in the granary rear chassis member. Note the thin iron support bracing rod running alongside the rear chassis member.

therefore may be advisable left to a hut specialist with experience to carry out the work.

As with all restoration work, once you start disturbing joints and replacing timbers, other unforeseen problems can start to occur. Take expert advice and don't rush things. In some instances, it may be prudent just to leave things alone as long as the original timbers appear to still be strong and in reasonably sound condition overall, preserve them with a good quality wood treatment, and live with any imperfections.

I have seen a repair carried out where the rear chassis member and joints have been in very poor condition. The rear floor had been supported by an additional wooden beam across the underneath of the floor, and then wooden spacers used between this beam and the iron rear axle, with the whole repair re- enforced by some strengthening ironwork. Although strong and well made, this is a classic case of a repair that will always look like a temporary repair, so major restoration work will eventually be necessary in order for the hut to be restored with the correct detailing it deserves.

Inspecting the body frame and corrugated sheeting

The framework of the granary was generally sound, although some work was needed to the bottom of the door frame where it attaches to the rear chassis beam. Accessibility to inspect and treat the framework is good as there is no internal matchboard panelling as with shepherds' huts.

On closer inspection, the original roof corrugated sheetings were quite rough around the edges, and also had a few holes, but a decision was made to preserve all of them as they were otherwise sound and weather proof. The front and rear ones were crucial to keep as there was writing on the inside of them, details being included later in the book. As the corners of the roof sheets (front and rear), were quite fragile in places, pieces of corrugation would eventually be cut and carefully inserted underneath the original ones to give additional support.

There is a strip of timber (approx.121 3/4" x 1/2" x 2 1/2") that runs along the top of the corrugated panels on both sides of the granary body, just under the roof overhang. These are called 'cover strips', and are included to stop wind blowing rain underneath the roof sheeting and into the hut interior. They were in reasonably sound condition and would just require an application of wood preservative. Farris huts that have interior wooden roof panelling do not require these timber cover strips as the panels usually protrude out a little under the roof overhang, thus preventing water from seeping in.

The rear corrugated sheet, adjacent to the door, had taken a bit of a battering during its life time and had a piece of off cut sheeting slid behind it to fill a large hole. Luckily, the rear piece of corrugated sheet on Farris huts overlaps the rear offside corner sheet by three corrugations, and butts against the iron door latch. By carefully removing the nails that secured the rear sheet, it might be possible to tidy and trim it to size with tin snips and move the sheet over slightly to make it look more presentable, thus retaining the original panel. Alternative options would be to patch the large hole again, which would look very tatty, or replace it with a completely new panel.

Inevitably, there are always very small areas of the side corrugation that have either corroded or been damaged over the years through abuse and neglect but do not warrant replacing a complete sheet. In these situations, it is often possible to slide a small piece of tin behind the original. This is useful where part of the timber frame, wooden panelling or chassis are exposed, in order to give some protection to them from the elements. Once painted, these small patched areas can look very acceptable and help to preserve as much of the original sheeting as possible.

A Special Event

I contacted Sybil during the summer of 2012 to see if she would be available to visit her old granary near Bere Regis to see its restoration progress to date, and at the same time have a look at another project, originally built by the John Farris company of Shaftesbury. This other hut was eventually going to appear on Amazing Spaces, Series 2 (Episode 8), on Channel 4 in 2013.

The John Farris hut is an early example also used for research and comparisons in this book. It had been found on a private estate near Winchester and has subsequently undergone quite an extensive restoration by shepherd's hut specialist, Eddie Butterfield of Bere Regis, Dorset. It required replacement chassis beams, axles and horse shafts, but retained its original body such as the framework, interior panelling, window, some of its floor, and corrugated sheeting, etc. Repairs to the old door, wood treatment, staining, polishing, preparation and painting of the body and wheels, the renovation and fitting of an original stove, and numerous other jobs would eventually be carried out by myself in order to help keep costs down.

The evening would consist of a small picnic for Sybil, including watching the partly restored John Farris shepherd's hut being coupled to a horse, using new ash shafts based on the originals, and being pulled down the road. Afterwards Sybil would inspect the granaries progress and see other makes of huts awaiting restoration.

Sybil was very pleased to be invited as a representative of the Farris family. I collected her from Coombe Bissett and drove her to a location near Bere Regis where the event was going to take place. On arrival, we did a quick detour to admire the steam engine and huge saw used for cutting the timber for the axles and chassis parts for shepherds' huts. I could already see Sybil's excitement and interest growing as she started reminiscing about how her father and grandfather would have felt,

Sybil admiring the steam engine.

Achellia enjoying the event.   *A record of Sybil's special day.*

seeing timbers cut in the same traditional way as they did at the Coombe Bissett Works all those years ago. There was no hesitation with this spritely 95 year old to climb out of my car and have her photograph taken next to this impressive machinery.

The steam engine was a French Marshall Britannia c.1910, and has a fascinating history as it was originally cut up during the Second World War (e.g. body, crankshaft, etc.) and hidden to prevent the Germans using it. After the war, it was carefully and professionally reassembled and welded back together and now used to power a huge vintage saw bench. The quality of its restoration is superb!

We then continued our trip to the premises where the event was to take place. Eddie Butterfield was the organiser and host. It had been arranged for a small television film crew to be present as they were intending to film the John Farris hut

J. Farris hut in tow.

for the Amazing Spaces Series, and Eddie had also organised an independent photographer to be present.

Sybil was 'guest of honour' and seemed to be thoroughly enjoying herself as she was introduced to everybody, and soon settled down in a chair to have a picnic and wait for this unique event to begin.

Eddie had also organised a friend to provide some 'horse power' that would be capable of towing the hut. A beautiful horse called Achellia soon arrived and was eventually coupled up to the wooden shafts ready for action.

An excellent reconstruction of the original shafts had been built by Eddie after hours were spent researching and discussing the finer detailing about them. Eddie even measured the horse to ensure they would fit snugly. We were fortunate that Sybil provided me with an old John Farris & Sons picture of some workers behind a banner which showed a set of shafts on a John Farris hut in the background.

As we were relaxing and watching all the preparation, Sybil asked me if I liked horses and seemed to agree that 'they were lovely at a safe distance'. Sybil has a certain wit and sense of humour that is infectious, so an enjoyable evening in her company was guaranteed. This particular horse is one of a team of four used professionally, and has featured in a few well known TV drama series.

Sybil inspecting the rear chassis beam. *Sybil checking the new front axle timbers.*

Various instructions were given, and slowly the horse set off with the shepherd's hut in tow, and cameras 'rolling'. It was an incredible sight, seeing it slowly and noisily moving along behind a beautiful and calm horse who appeared to be enjoying all the fuss and attention. One starts to realise the enormity of a horse having to tow such a large and heavy weight, and how slow and difficult this must have been when huts were originally being transported to different locations for shepherds to use during the lambing season.

The owners of the Chestnut Dutch Gelderlander remarked that they 'would usually use four horses when towing a carriage of a similar weight', although it was coping quite comfortably pulling the shepherd's hut over such a short distance. We are indebted for their kindness in providing their gorgeous horse for this special occasion. The advantages of steam engines and tractors became very apparent whilst watching this reconstruction of horse power towing a hut, but the beauty and character of the horse gave a certain ambience to the occasion and allowed reflection of how these hard working animals were used years ago.

The enjoyment on Sybil's face watching and experiencing one of her great uncles shepherds' houses being towed by a horse, approximately 130 years after it had originally been built, made the evening very special and rewarding, and we are indebted to her for agreeing to attend this unique event.

We then strolled into the barn where Sybil's old hut was being repaired. She looked amazed at the various models (one displaying a Titt & Co. name plate) that were standing alongside her old granary, awaiting restoration.

Sybil was then shown the replacement wooden front axle beams alongside the rotten ones, and new rear chassis beam. These had been cut and were shortly to be fitted to the granary. She also examined the water damage to the rear chassis beam, now visible as the rear floorboards had been removed. Sybil appeared to be extremely interested in its progress and was soon happily having her photo taken as a record for the occasion.

The evenings event was gradually coming to an end, and as I was very aware that Sybil may start to feel tired, I felt it was a good time to say our farewells and drive her home. On the way back, the two of us were engrossed in conversation about George and John Farris. Sybil recalled a trip to the Shaftesbury works with her father, who was shown around her great uncle's premises and appeared to have found it very interesting. It would certainly have been an occasion to remember, considering the difficulties between their families years before.

She was also very keen to point out the Blandford Road site where Charles and Nelly moved to shortly before the Coombe Bissett works closed. This is situated at the opposite end of the village to her grandfather's old premises, and the house and workshop are still there and owned by Farris relatives.

I dropped Sybil off at her home realising that the evening had been a 'once in a lifetime experience' for a Farris enthusiast, and hopefully for Sybil as well.

Eddie later remarked that 'for Sybil to have witnessed her great uncle's old hut being towed by a horse, as it would have been, was something to behold'. I couldn't have put it better myself!

Sybil, Rollin and Eddie.

Completing the restoration

Sybil's granary eventually arrived at its new home, in July 2013, and was positioned carefully in my meadow ready for final restoration and preservation work to be carried out. The arrival of it was long overdue, as distractions on the John Farris restoration had somehow taken priority due to the time schedule of its filming and TV appearance.

Wood treatment

One of the first jobs was to preserve the woodwork and liberally apply wood treatment to all timbers, including chassis, axles, interior framework, floor, door and steps.

Because the rear chassis beam had been replaced, the rear floorboards had not been hammered back into position, thereby enabling a good application of preservative to be easily applied into some of the usually inaccessible places. The floorboards could then be put back using traditional type forged nails as required. Three old replacement boards were used nearest the doorway as substitutes for the worn originals.

The section of the main chassis beam at the rear left side looked a little damaged, but it was still strong enough to support the new rear chassis member. The nearside door frame that attaches into this joint also needed some attention. Rather than renew the whole frame or 'cut in' a visible replacement piece, I decided to make an 'L' shaped section in hardwood. The horizontal part of the 'L' neatly fitted into the chassis joint, whilst the longer vertical piece was glued into a cut out section on the rear part of the original door frame.

A recycled piece of timber was cut to size (e.g. 73 1/4" x 2 3/4" x 1" thick) and used to replace the original rotten strip that was attached to the outer part of the door frame. Once wood preserver had been applied, it was then secured into position, thereby hiding any repairs, and the rear corner of the corrugated sheeting could eventually be tidied and nailed back into position over the wood.

Another problem encountered was where the lower internal horizontal beam (used to lean sacks against) attaches to the nearside door frame. The beam was originally nailed into position and now required additional support and wood treatment as it had twisted and deteriorated slightly. A rusty heavy duty wrought iron bracket discovered on an old railway sleeper looked authentic, and was found to fit perfectly under the beam, and has been fitted using old large square headed nuts. The beam was also showing signs of a crack a short distance from the doorway, so some glue was forced into it and everything was clamped together. Another pitted bracket was found and cut to size using an angle grinder and chamfered slightly on the end, then screwed into the beam, using steel screws, to provide rigidity. Both repairs look as if they were done years ago and therefore blend in well.

It was also necessary to replace the offside of the doorframe whilst fitting the new rear chassis beam as the joints were also damaged. The door is attached to this side of the frame and therefore needed to be very sturdy and sound.

Although it's important to follow original detailing carefully, there are occasions when it may be sensible to consider using screws as an alternative to nails during a restoration. A good example is where an old chassis may be slightly damaged in places and may suffer unforeseen problems such as increased splitting due to hammering large nails into it. I find drilling a small 'pilot' hole for a largish nail can be helpful in both new and old timbers to help avoid damage, but an overall assessment needs to be carried out before work commences.

The ends of the rear axle still needed attention as gluing and clamping of the cracks had not been successful. The wood kept springing back into its existing position once the clamps were released. A coloured polyurethane wood glue (30

Rear chassis beam joint.

minute setting time) was therefore used to glue and seal any cracks. This type of glue allows for expansion of the wood in wet and dry weather conditions, and although it's a modern rather than a traditional product, it should help to preserve the original rear axle for quite a few more years before any further maintenance is required. It's also useful where cracks have developed in the axles or chassis in order to prevent water collecting, although it is best to use it selectively.

As previously mentioned, the timber framework is not easily accessible in shepherds' houses due to the design consisting of corrugated sheets on the outside, and wooden panelling (matchboarding) on the inside. However, for nature lovers, the gap in between provides a wonderful 'paradise' for spiders and other creepy crawlies that take up residence and sneak out in the middle of the night whilst you are asleep!

My poem *Lurking Bodies* was inspired by some of these creatures found in the granary during its restoration.

Where panelling is present, it's important to treat it sympathetically. My own preference is to leave and preserve it in as close to 'as found condition' as possible. For example, if the bottom part of a panel, or edge of the floor, has been chewed by a rat, consider not repairing it unless it is seriously damaged. It's all part of its history and just adds to the character.

Access to the framework was not a problem with the granary due to the absence of the matchboarding. Where accessibility to the framework is difficult on panelled shepherds' houses, one needs to evaluate if it's necessary to remove any of the exterior sheeting for a wood treatment to be applied. In this instance, where sheeting needs to be replaced, this obviously gives a good opportunity to carry out treatment to the body frame. Removal of the sheeting nails can be a problem as sometimes they bend or snap (particularly the thin type) so care should be taken in order that as many of the original can be reused. Where original nails are not reusable, it's often possible to reuse the washers.

Wood preserving timbers has to be one of the most unpleasant jobs during a restoration, but is an important consideration in order to prevent further infestations of woodworm and to help preserve new and existing timbers against future rot and decay. Choose carefully, as it's essential to treat the timbers rather than coat them in something that just repels water and colours the wood!

If deciding to use a wood treatment, use some form of protective clothing, gloves, suitable mask and goggles, which are essential for Health and Safety reasons. Always follow the manufacturers instructions!

Although a very disagreeable and time consuming task (I dislike using chemical wood treatments immensely), it is actually quite a relief when it is completed knowing that the wood treatment will help to preserve the timbers for a number of years. The height of a Farris bodywork, with wheels attached, does allow for easy access to apply a preservative to the chassis, axles and underneath floor area, and hopefully only these areas will require a periodic application in the future.

I usually use a clear wood treatment, especially on original interior timbers, but some that have a light colour can look acceptable on the chassis, axles and under the floorboards if desired. I adopted this method to help blend timber colours on the exterior wood of the granary, such as the replacement front axle, with reasonable results.

As a guide, a restorer can expect to use at least a couple of gallons (approx. 9 to 10 litres) of wood treatment when liberally applied by brush to the exterior timbers, such as axles, chassis, steps and under the floorboards. A similar quantity of treatment may also be required on the interior framework, panelling (as applicable), floor, door, roof timber apex ends, etc. Obviously, a large shepherd's hut with interior panelling will require slightly larger quantities of preservative than a smaller granary without matchboard panels.

Traditionally, a preservative such as a wood tar would probably have been used on exterior timbers such as the chassis and wooden axles to give protection against the weather. Lead paint was another option used, and remnants of paint can sometimes be noticed on original axles.

Cleaning & Preserving

It was necessary to clean the granary interior to remove excessive grime, dirt and cobwebs. A damp cloth and bucket of water was used with a 'splash' of something I found under our kitchen sink. Sugar soap is said to be a good product for this purpose. Once the interior had been cleaned and dried thoroughly, a clear wood treatment was applied to all the interior timbers and a clear beeswax was eventually used to protect and seal the wood.

Clear beeswax is very useful for unpainted timbers as it helps to fill in any woodworm holes, and nourishes the wood without dramatically altering the timber colour. It can give exceptionally good results when applied to interior panelling. A darker wax is also useful, but should be used sparingly.

I have also seen products such as teak oil used, but this tends to make the inside look quite dark, so Danish or linseed oils are probably more preferable options. Always do a small 'sample area' first to check the colour shade.

Personally, I prefer a traditional clear beeswax on internal timbers. Adding a little turpentine to beeswax may be worth considering to help it absorb thoroughly into the wood, thereby giving deep lasting protection. A light buff with a clean cloth once its dried is all that is required to retain a natural finish.

Be careful when purchasing some beeswax products as they are not as natural as one would presume, and include harmful additives which can be dangerous to ones health.

With shepherds' houses that have had interior panelling painted, it is possible to create a finish that does not look too new and blends with the overall aged character of the restoration. A two tone effect (e.g. the ceiling and half way down the panelling one colour, bottom half a different colour) can look very good. With original huts, I find it pleasant to enter them and feel that a shepherd has just popped out to tend his flock, rather than entering one that has just undergone a modern 'makeover', although I do appreciate that everyone's tastes are different. Water based paints are ideal for this purpose.

If there is historical evidence, such as pencil markings (e.g. dates, signatures and numbers) scribbled on the interior woodwork from previous occupants, shepherds or even the craftsmen who originally built the hut, it would be advisable to leave these areas undisturbed in order to retain its unique history. Over enthusiastic treatment and waxing could cause original markings to fade or disappear. Some form of protection against damage to these jottings may also be advisable, but could detract from the overall character of the interior.

Indeed, I have yet to climb up the steps into an original shepherd's house or granary that does not have its own distinct atmosphere, and feels completely individual and different to other examples made by Farris or their competitors. To then discover evidence of hand written notes, numbers or even dates written in its interior is incredibly exciting and stimulating, and contributes to the overall uniqueness that one experiences in these special living spaces.

Preparation and painting the body

Regarding the roof, I felt there was no huge advantage in replacing any of the original corrugated roofing sheets. The corners were in poor condition at both the front and the rear of the hut, but the roof was still watertight, and overall in reasonable condition. Strengthening of the corners should suffice as I could live with any rough edges along the front and rear ends of the roof.

A bit of 'fettling' of the original corrugation such as trimming rotten bits with tin snips, and shaping with a panel beaters hammer were necessary. Reinforcement of the corners was achieved by cutting pieces from an old corrugated panel to the required sizes, carefully loosening the roof nails as required, and sliding a piece under each of the original sheets at each corner of the roof. A leather hammer, a tyre lever and a straight and sturdy piece of timber were exceedingly useful for this purpose. Slots were made in the pieces to be inserted under the original roof panels so as to correspond to where the roof nails were positioned. The corrugation could then be slid into place and then held by the original nails once they were tapped back down.

A few small nuts, bolts and washers were then used to secure the original corrugation and newly inserted pieces in place near the roof edges. Tiny holes were drilled as required, bolts inserted and secured (a fiddle of a job), then the top of them were filed so as to make them less obvious. They would be virtually hidden once bitumen had been applied to seal the roof. Mild steel rivets (peened over) may also be suitable for this purpose, but blind rivets (e.g. aluminium pop rivets) should be avoided as they look too modern.

Although not perfect, it has enabled the original roof sheets to be preserved. This is very important with the granary as there is no interior matchboarding to hide any new or recycled sheeting that could have been used, which may not exactly match the

Preparation & painting of the corrugated sheeting.

original. Because there was 'evidence of the past' written on a couple of the roof sheets on the inside, preserving the genuine sheeting was essential.

A rub down with a stiff brush and a couple of coats of black bitumen on the outside would give a reasonable finish. In time, the roof would dull to a matt finish which looks good and very much in keeping with a sympathetic restoration, and any age related holes or rough edges would just add to the overall individuality.

Its quite common for roofs needing to be replaced due to the original one being in very poor condition. It's important to ensure new sheets are of the correct size and have the same overhang, including the front and rear ends, as slightly oversized sheets can look out of proportion.

Painting the roof in bitumen, rather than gloss, has the advantage of looking authentic as well as a good sealant against wet weather. Cleaning under the overhang of the corrugated roof and applying a wax or oil product is also worth considering, especially if rust is present.

Some of the internal edges of the side panels were also showing signs of rust, especially where the hessian had been, so these areas were cleaned and preserved accordingly. Without wanting to advertise too many brand names, an automobile product with words similar to 'wax and oil' are excellent for this purpose.

The corrugated sides had been painted green during Sybil's ownership so were in fairly sound condition overall. Angela commented that the granary 'was in a dreadful state, having been used to store chicken food in a farmyard for about forty years'. Sybil wanted the granary improved so the corrugation was painted green. It had previously been covered in what appeared to be a black tar substance which needed to be removed and would have been a difficult task.

It's worth noting the health implications of trying to remove old materials such as tar, pitch or bitumen. A face mask (e.g. British Standard), industrial rubber gloves and suitable eye protection are essential items when carrying out this process.

Work in progress.

The rear corrugation was causing some concern and looked a little tatty with a large hole in it. I wanted to keep as much of the original sheeting as possible so it was carefully removed and tidied with some tin snips. I also find an electric hand grinder helpful when cutting corrugated sheeting to size, but these useful tools need to be treated with respect as they are dangerous and can be too vicious for the more delicate tasks.

A decision was then made to turn the corrugation around 180 degrees and slide it behind the adjacent corner sheet, where the door latch is positioned. It was then secured in place with the original nails. No hole or rough edges were now evident, and I was very pleased with the outcome.

It can sometimes be a difficult decision whether to renew corrugated sheeting even when they are in very poor condition. Dents are not usually a problem as they add character, but sheets that are rotten and brittle will require some attention and may need replacing. My preference is to retain and preserve as much of the original as possible, although one has to be realistic as to whether the existing corrugation is capable of keeping the rain out and does not cause a problem later on. It is possible in certain situations, to patch a small damaged area (e.g. a hole) by inserting a piece of galvanised sheeting behind, and once painted, it can blend in reasonably well.

With every dent, tear, crease and hole, there is a story, a mystery and even a memory. Something easily forgotten when restoring part of our heritage back to its former glory. Ideally, aim for a certain ruggedness and ambience that a sympathetic restoration can achieve, which is often lost with over restored examples.

Continuing with the restoration, I decided to insert a piece of corrugated off-cut that I had cut to size to the rear nearside, lower corner of the bodywork, due to it being damaged. This was more preferable than replacing the whole sheet. I resisted the temptation to remove too much of the original distorted corrugation, applying a minimalistic approach, thereby sliding the prepared off-cut under the existing panel. It's not perfect, but the original corrugated sheeting has been preserved, and the repair helps to provide some protection against the weather for part of the chassis and framework.

Careful preparation of all the exterior corrugation with sandpaper and a wire brush to remove any loose rust and flaking paint, usually provides a sound 'keyed' surface ready for the application of a suitable primer and a couple of top coats of paint. The panels on the granary however, proved a little more tedious as dampness unfortunately had penetrated under the paintwork and the sheeting required the majority of existing paint to be removed with the additional aid of a scraper.

Although a time consuming and laborious task, a reasonable surface for painting would eventually be achievable. I tend to use a medium grade paper when sanding the exterior body (and woodwork), reducing to a finer grade as necessary. When applying paint, a fine grade 'wet & dry' sandpaper with a dash of washing up liquid in a bucket of water is excellent for removing any excessive runs and blemishes in the paintwork in-between coats.

Gloss paint enhances any defects, especially when viewed closely, so don't expect perfection. My main aim with the preparation is to ensure that the paint adheres well and gives a reasonable finish overall. It's really disheartening if ones hard work ends in blistering and flaking of paint after a few years due to not preparing the surface thoroughly beforehand.

Although a purist at heart, and enjoy seeing corrugated sheeting left in an 'as found condition', I find preparing and painting a hut quite a satisfying experience for obvious reasons such as overall appearance, protection of original sheeting from the elements, and keeping my wife happy!!!

A shade of green always appears very satisfactory as it blends well within the countryside that I am fortunate to live in. However, I have felt a little more adventurous with Sybil's granary as it has a certain provenance about it, and I decided after much deliberation to paint the corrugation in black gloss. This can be extremely unforgiving on old dented corrugated surfaces as it greatly accentuates any blemishes and faults. It can sometimes also look a little austere, but in some instances may provide some panache and style. With a contrasting colour for the wheels, it would certainly make the granary stand out from the crowd, very much like its previous owner, Sybil.

Areas showing signs of rust can always be treated with a rust inhibitor chemical after preparation (e.g. sandpapering) before applying a suitable primer and top coat. If leaving the corrugation in an 'as found condition', it's advisable to avoid these rust treatments, as a chemical reaction occurs and the metal turns black. In this situation, it's preferable to carefully clean the panel with a wire-brush and sandpaper, and apply an oil or wax product as an alternative form of preservation.

The granary still had signs of where black tar or pitch had been present, so as a precaution it was decided to use an aluminium primer to give better adhesion for the top coats.

In some instances, where the corrugated sides are painted with a tar like substance and a different coloured top coat is required, it may be worth seeing if an aluminium primer will successfully adhere to the top of the old surface without reacting, thereby allowing for an alternative type of paint and colour to be used. I have found that tar like products needs to be very old and hard for this to usually be successful, with numerous flaws and crazing in the overall finish to be expected if this approach is adopted. In my experience, I have generally had no problems with adhesion of coats of paint when using an aluminium primer but perhaps I have just been lucky!

Where old corrugated sheets have signs of lichen and moss, it's important to brush it off and wash with water and a splash of bleach to help provide a sound surface for painting. Allow to dry thoroughly before a final rinse with water.

Using a top-quality exterior oil based paint suitable for metal surfaces (applied with a good brush) is worth the additional expense due to its durability and finish, although there can be less options with choice of colour shades. Spraying is also worth considering if one has suitable facilities.

Painting with a brush is my preferred method as it feels more traditional and is generally easier to use in outdoor conditions. The finish also looks more authentic as there will inevitably be unavoidable brush marks and numerous imperfections in the paintwork.

Very good results can be achieved by spraying, but one needs to be careful that the overall finish doesn't resemble a brand new hut. I have seen one example which had been fitted with new corrugated sheeting and painted to an incredibly high standard by someone exceedingly efficient with a spray gun. The hut also had an old name plate fitted, but because it appeared so immaculate, one could be excused for wondering if it was actually original or a reproduction.

It's worth noting that new galvanised corrugated sheeting will require a special primer used for non ferrous metals.

If in doubt, research any new products and take recommendations from a knowledgeable paint specialist. It can save you time and money. Always adhere to any Health & Safety instructions or advice as applicable!

Preparation and painting always takes a lot longer than expected. Many enthusiasts won't have the comfort of a barn to work in during a restoration and are therefore very dependant on good weather conditions. With the granary, concentrating on sections of the corrugation during dry spells has been essential, leaving other tasks for slightly more unsettled days. Carefully painting one panel with a top coat of gloss paint can easily take 25 minutes to brush on. Removing unsightly runs considerably longer! Taking into account the general preparation of individual sheets, priming and at least a couple of top coats of gloss, one starts to realise the enormity of the task in hand. In addition, one also has the height of the hut to contend with!

My own experiences with problems of painting are reflected in the number of insects that decide to glue themselves to the paintwork on a warm sunny day, or struggling with more adverse weather such as wind, rain and damp conditions. Even the sunshine warms up the corrugated panels causing paint to dry too quickly. Perhaps I should consider investing in a barn to make life easier and to achieve better results, but another shepherd's hut would be far more desirable.

Painting the wheels

The wheels on Sybil's granary had previously been painted in 'red lead' paint under Sybil's instructions. As Angela commented 'Mum wanted them done with red lead paint, because she said that's what they always used'. Well, if anyone would know, it would be Sybil, as she remembers the wheels being made at her grandfather's foundry.

It was therefore decided to apply a coat of red oxide primer to touch up any chips and scratches. With much debate and apprehension, a decision was also made to give a couple of top coats of light blue. As previously mentioned, George Farris wheels can occasionally show remnants of a blue paint on them, so a similar colour was chosen for Sybil's granary wheels.

Although Sybil confirms wheels were sometimes painted in red lead paint, as this would help preserve them and contribute to their attractiveness, evidence of a blue paint found during restorations of George's huts does suggest that some of their wheels may also have been finished in blue. In addition, remnants of blue found behind the cast iron name plate (e.g. on the plate and wooden end boarding) also provide additional evidence of this colour paint periodically being used. Pigments break down over the years making remaining shades of blue useful as a guide rather than an exact colour.

One can only speculate as to whether George Farris may have offered at some stage a blue paint as an option, or whether it could, on the odd occasion, have been applied by individual customers at a later date. The fact that remnants of blue can sometimes be discovered behind the name plate suggests that it was possibly the foundry!

Interestingly, remnants of blue paint was also found on one of the granary rear axle castings. The colour was not too dissimilar to the blue paint used to re paint its wheels. Certainly, blue wheels look good and the colour helps to define their attractive lines.

Black paint, pitch or anything that was suitable and available would also have been used by hut makers during the 19th century. Whether John Farris painted his wheels

Detailing of granary rear wheel hub & cap.

in a particular colour is unclear.

These days, unpainted Farris wheels can look good if left in a rusty looking condition and can be coated with an oil or wax type product if desired. It was decided that the rest of the ironwork on Sybil's granary was to be left in this rusty finish as it looks very authentic and not over restored.

Attaching the granary name plate

The original Farris name plate was attached above the door with coach bolts, rather than screws, to make it a little more secure. This was a very satisfying moment as it instantly gave the granary its identity! Again, a wax was applied after cleaning it, so as to retain its character. Sometimes name plates are beautifully restored and repainted, but keeping name plates looking old and in an 'as found condition' can look quite appealing. Polishing with stove blackening paste also gives a pleasing result and can then also be lightly waxed or oiled to add additional protection against the elements. It can be a real fine line when restoring a historic hut, as it's easy to get carried away and end up with a result that looks almost brand new. There is no doubt that some enthusiasts and restorers want to achieve this, but it is worth remembering to aim for a restoration which still retains some of the characteristics of a late 19th and early 20th century creation. Easier said than done, but by using traditional materials and methods, and some experimentation and personal restraint, a reasonable authentic finish can usually be achieved successfully without spoiling the overall ambience that one would expect from a successful rebuild.

Luckily, restorations do mellow with age, including newly painted surfaces, and if decorated sympathetically with features such as period furniture, shepherd related items, possibly hessian matting or sacking on the floor, and even pretty curtains and other soft furnishings, a little extra comfort can be provided and enjoyed whilst keeping within the boundaries of acceptable 19th century criteria.

Certainly, in the case of Sybil's hut, an authentic restoration that retains its character as a historic portable granary is a priority, with a touch of individualism and personality introduced, as it is hoped that it will be preserved and enjoyed for future generations to come.

Restored & displayed in its natural environment.

Lurking Bodies

Climbing the hut steps with a little trepidation,
Feeling your way, 'cause the darkness of the night,
Musty smell and dust to greet you,
Bodies lurking, ready to give you a fright.

Discomfort of cobwebs sticking to your face,
Wiping them away at an alarming rate,
Starting to feel itchy all over your body,
Tiredness sets in, it's starting to get late.

Shivering under the worn hessian blanket,
Trying to get some sleep in this dismal place,
Flickers of light from the candle beside you,
Emerging bodies appearing with haste.

Exaggerated forms in the twilight hours,
Watching from the ceiling with a menacing stance,
Sucking of blood their speciality,
Still very hungry, waiting for a chance.

Feeling uncomfortable, tossing and turning,
Bodies have been feasting all night long,
Eyes now open, glancing all around you,
Insects retreated, they have now all gone.

A paradise for creepy crawlies in a hut so old,
Wandering freely across the wooden floor,
Gaps between the corrugation, a place to ponder?
Becoming a nuisance, that's for sure.

Dog chewing on an unfortunate specimen,
A tiny rodent caught without a fight,
Hidden under his blanket, seemingly forever,
The remains disgusting, but an enjoyable bite.

Shepherds' huts consisting of tiny spaces,
Many a haven, for creatures so small,
Treasured by a few, despised by others,
Lurking bodies, scurrying around for ever more.

Rollin

Inspired by the creepy crawlies found lurking in Sybil's hut

George Farris name plates

Finding any restoration project with its original cast iron name plate is always very exciting as it helps to identify the manufacturer and in some instances helps to estimate the huts age more accurately. I do know of the odd case where a restoration has been completed and the missing name plate has been replaced with a similar one found at a rally or auction, which may not have been identical to the one it originally displayed, making a slightly misleading compromise. Other enthusiasts with similar huts may then presume theirs should also have the same type of plate.

As enthusiasts, we all understand the emotions of wanting to find an original name plate to display on our huts, but from a historic perspective, perhaps one has to question the wisdom of attaching an incorrect one. It's certainly an area worth careful consideration and thought.

One could also argue that it's better to have an original, albeit wrong Farris name plate attached to a genuine Farris hut, as it's reuniting a plate that would have been cast at the foundry all those years ago, and it's more preferable than having a replica casting made.

Reproduction Farris name plates have also been produced and fitted to Farris huts, which can also contribute to the overall confusion when identifying the model and trying to estimate an approximate year of manufacture.

The range of original name plates that I have seen on unrestored George Farris huts is small, with three shapes in particular appearing consistent.

1. Large Rectangular

The granary displays a large and heavy cast iron name plate (e.g. rectangular shape) believed by Sybil to be of the earlier type, stating 'G Farris Maker Coombe Bissett Nr Salisbury'. Sybil previously mentioned that 'the earlier name plates had G, for George on them'.

The early plate size is 11" x 6 3/8" x 3/4" thick, on the outer edge. Fortunately Angela removed the heavy cast iron one from the granary when the wood it was screwed to needed replacing, and to avoid it being stolen. The granary example is black, with evidence of remnants of gold highlighting the raised letters and the surrounding front outer edge.

These large name plates were also used on George's smaller 8 ft x 6 ft and 12 ft x 6 ft huts during the same period that the granary was built and had thick wheel hubs, with eight spokes on the front wheels and ten spokes on the rear. The interior curved wooden roof support was of the thin design.

Whether there was an earlier name plate before this rectangular design of George's is unclear, and one can only speculate if the very earliest Farris huts would have had one at all. It is likely that when John went into competition against George, there would have been a necessity for both brothers to advertise their names on their own shepherds' houses and portable granaries sometime during the mid to late 1880's. In addition, other manufactures were beginning to produce their own similar designed huts around this period of time, and advertising their own names on them accordingly. The rectangular name plate clearly states 'G' for George, and is large and heavy, as one would expect of a late Victorian or early Edwardian casting on a hut. George's later examples omitted the initial G, and were generally smaller and lighter in design. Nevertheless, there were some smaller name plates made that included the letter 'G' which are of a size usually found on items such as agricultural implements of this period. I have also seen a narrow rectangular plate with a 'G' attached to a couple of shepherds' huts, which I will briefly discuss shortly.

2. Oval

An oval name plate, cast with 'Farris, Maker, Coombe, Salisbury', was also attached to some of George's shepherds' houses. Because there is no 'G' in the name, we can presume they are not earlier models. The plate size is 5 3/4" x 3". A hut studied (approx. 12 ft x 6 ft) did not have the usual Farris spoked wheels with hub caps. The internal curved roof support was of the deeper design similar to many of George's later examples. This name plate is quite rare to find on a Farris hut, but a number are known to exist.

3. Oblong

An oblong shaped name plate with the words 'Farris, Maker, Coombe, Salisbury' was also displayed on some of George's shepherds' houses. The plate size is 7 3/4" x 4 1/8" x 3/8" thick. An example researched had ten spokes on both front and rear wheels, and a deep curved wooden internal roof support.

It is unclear if the oblong name plate preceded the oval name plate on George's huts, as both appear to have the deeper internal roof supports and overall similar characteristics. There were however, a few subtle differences between the different models examined, notably the width of their internal matchboarding. My intuition is suggesting possibilities, and I could surmise about my thoughts on this matter, but perhaps it is better to wait until I have more evidence!

An interesting observation of the above name plates usually found on George's huts is that all three examples have the word 'MAKER' included.

Other name plates

Sybil did suggest that there was a possibility that a name plate with G. Farris & Sons may also have been cast, but she wasn't absolutely certain. No doubt other plates could also have been used on George's huts, but ideally, unrestored examples need to be discovered (or early photos) in order to provide this evidence accurately.

Another cast iron name plate that I have examined showed 'G. Farris Coombe Salisbury'. It was oblong in shape, and its size was 7 5/8" x 4 1/4" x 3/8" thick. The enthusiast who owned it highlighted the 'G' as a 'C', but he was not sure if it was correct. I showed Sybil a photo who confirmed it would definitely have been a 'G'. Whether this plate was ever included on a hut is unknown, but it could have originally been on an agricultural implement.

A narrow rectangular cast plate (size 8 3/4" x 2") stating 'G. Farris, Coombe Bissett' and displayed on a couple of sympathetically restored huts were exciting finds.

These huts were very unusual as they were longer and wider than the standard full size Farris shepherds' houses that I am familiar with. The approximate external size of one of the huts that I measured was 13ft 2 3/4" long x 7ft 3 1/2" wide.

One example differed to the other as the door was on the offside of the rear of the body and it seemed to have a different axle assembly and wheels that one usually associates with George's huts. The interiors of both closely resembled the characteristics of a Farris construction with similar internal bracing.

The other example had Farris style wheels with ten spokes on the front and rear (the front wheel hubs appeared thicker than the usual ten spoke ones seen on some Farris huts that I have researched) and a rare front axle turntable stating 'Farris

Coombe Salisbury'. The turntable was without a 'G' suggesting it may not be from an early example. The internal wooden roof support measured 6" deep on this shepherd's house, which is more usual on later Farris huts.

These are extremely interesting shepherds' huts requiring further research and investigation, and to be clarified in my ongoing research.

Dating George Farris huts from their name plates alone is not that obvious, but my research suggests that there could possibly be a link with the number of spokes in the front wheels, with a familiar pattern materialising with examples investigated. There also appears to be some consistency with the huts curved interior roof supports.

For example, Sybil's early granary has a large heavy rectangular name plate that corresponds to eight spokes in the front wheels. The same plate on some of George's smaller and larger huts also have identical wheels and name plates as Sybil's granary. In addition, the unrestored examples examined had a narrow curved wooden internal roof support. A large rectangular name plate with eight spoked front wheels and narrow internal roof support generally appears synonymous with an earlier model!

However, I have noticed variations with a couple of restored huts that need further investigation. One had two narrow curved roof supports, the other a deeper roof support! Both had the early large rectangular castings with a 'G' and eight spoked front wheels. These huts could be examples where a change in roof support design was implemented.

A few of George's later huts without a 'G' that I have examined had wheels with ten spokes on the front and rear. An example by John Farris & Sons was also found to have an identical spoke count. As discussed before, the hubs on the front wheels with ten spokes appear to be less bulky than front wheels with eight spokes. George's later huts also tend to have the deeper curved wooden internal roof support. My observations of other Farris examples with additional spokes in the front wheels are indicating a possible modification in their wheel design, and is certainly an area for future study. No doubt there will be exceptions!

As previously mentioned, Sybil does recall watching these wheels being cast in her grandfather's foundry and has subsequently suggested that wheels with additional spokes in their front wheels could have been an 'improvement in design'. Sybil also commented that the original wheel foundry mouldings were offered to a museum by Florrie (Thomas's daughter) during the late 1950's, but she was unsure exactly what happened to them.

Interestingly, George Farris huts can also be discovered with completely different types of cast wheels, without their traditional thin wrought iron spokes. It is unclear as to whether either of the Farris brothers changed to an alternative design of wheel at a later date, although this could be a possibility.

There is certainly inconsistency with a small amount of the George Farris shepherds' houses that I have examined, as I have seen different wheels in cast iron with six (one example with eight) broad spokes in the design. Similar cast iron wheels were certainly used by some of Farris's competitors.

There are definitely instances where genuine spoked Farris wheels have been replaced, over the years, by an alternative style, due to general wear and tear of the originals resulting in fractures and damage. We are looking at huts often over one hundred years old! The time factor and cost of repair may have proved restrictive, so a different wheel from another manufacturer would have sufficed. A hut may also have been found without wheels attached and had replacements fitted during a restoration. There could be all sorts of explanations.

These days, genuine Farris wheels in any condition are worth the expense of repairing because of their rarity. Due to a few similarities in hut design from some of Farris's competitors, their distinctive wheels, with wrought iron spokes, are one of the key factors and clues in helping to identify one of George's or John's huts when discovered.

Having said that, it's important not to presume that because a hut has the familiar Farris iron spoked wheels that it is definitely a Farris hut. Unfortunately it's not as simple as that, as wheels on other historic huts also get swopped and changed over the years, especially if it has previously undergone a restoration or has had a very hard life. New builds can also be found on occasion with genuine Farris wheels fitted, so it's important not to make quick presumptions with ones analysis. Other detailing, particularly to the chassis, axles, corrugated sheeting, general ironwork and interior also needs to be taken into consideration when an assessment is made.

Without doubt, Farris wheels are an area for further research in order to help clarify my observations and thoughts on the subject more clearly. It's certainly debatable why Farris would change their wheel design to ten spokes with thinner hubs on the front, whilst retaining thicker hubs on the rear. Perhaps increased commercial restraints could have been an influencing factor with the wheel design changes on some of their later huts. It may be that one can only realistically speculate on possible change in wheel design, but the consistency of some of the huts examined definitely encourages the desire for further investigation.

Birds regularly visit this G. Farris hut.

George Farris Huts

The following photo's show a selection of George's huts that were made at the Coombe Bissett Steam Plough Works.

Above, a restored G. Farris hut now used as a holiday retreat.

Before, during and after restoration. Large rectangular name plate (G. Farris). Body Size (external) 8ft x 6ft approx. This is an unusually small George Farris shepherd's hut complete with window. The example in the photo was panelled inside but had no stove. It was discovered in unrestored condition not far from the Coombe Bissett foundry. More research is required on this early small model for accurate detailing.

Photographs J.L.

Two images above: Oval name plate (G. Farris).
Body size (external) 12ft x 6 ft approx.
An uncommon and slightly later shepherd's hut.
This example is owned by an enthusiast in Dorset.
Larger windows and replacement wheels have been
added over the years.

G. Farris hut
requiring restoration.

Large rectangular name plate (G. Farris).
Body Size (external) 12ft x 6ft approx.
This large shepherd's hut is usually
easier to discover than the
smaller models, and gave
considerably more room
for a shepherd to live
in during lambing
time.

115

Oblong name plate (G. Farris). A very cosy interior. Body size (external) 12ft x 6ft approx. A Farris hut which is becoming increasingly hard to find. The example shown has ten spokes on both front and rear wheels plus an original oak floor.

Oblong name plate (G. Farris).
Body size (external)
12ft x 6ft approx.

John Farris Name Plates

The range of original name plates that I have seen on unrestored John Farris shepherds' huts is small, with three or four types appearing the norm. However, John Farris & Sons did provide a large range of name plates that appeared on other agricultural machinery and implements manufactured at their foundry. Such plates sometimes included addition names such as Favourite, Rex and Ace which referred to their chicken hutches, and were attached accordingly.

1. Circular

(late 19th century).
Some early John Farris shepherds' houses had a circular name plate, stating 'John Farris, The Belle Vue Works, Shaftesbury'. The plate size is 8" across x 1/4" thick. These name plates also had in their centre a small outline which may have been included to represent the 'Crest of Shaftesbury'.

Huts had either wooden front and rear axle beams, wooden front axle and wrought iron rear axle, or iron axles front and rear. Wheels had eight spokes on the front, and ten spokes on the rear.

2. Horseshoe

(late 19th century).
Other Shepherds' huts that I have researched had a name plate which was in the shape of a horseshoe, stating 'J. Farris, Shaftesbury'. The plate is approximately 9 1/2" deep (including the mounting points) and a few inches wider overall. The horseshoe ends point downwards. For the superstitious, whether this is good luck or bad luck is

a matter of personal opinion. A horseshoe with ends pointing upwards symbolises good energy stored and collected. Pointed downwards, good energy is lost, or arguably releases energy and luck to people around it.

All huts researched had iron axles front and rear. Front wheels also had eight spokes, and rear wheels had ten spokes.

3. Rectangular

(early 20th century).

Another hut researched was thought to date from around the early 1920's. Its original small rectangular name plate stated 'Agents J. Farris & Sons Shaftesbury'. The addition of 'Sons' on the name plate is particularly helpful in classifying this example as a later addition sold by the John Farris company. The word 'Agents' however, causes one to contemplate, as it suggests they are selling someone else's hut. John Farris & Sons were certainly agents selling other people's products, although it's not thought that they sold other makers huts. A convenient name plate could possibly have been taken 'off the shelf' and fitted onto one of their huts, and although probably a reasonable explanation, I have no firm evidence of this.

This example had the usual features of one of John's shepherds' huts but had replacement wooden axle beams with the usual chassis to axle deep wooden spacers associated with this design. An original small sliding window opened towards the rear of the hut. The interior had many pencil jottings and dates on the wooden panelling depicting the number of sheep counted by the shepherd, including a date from the 1920's. Interestingly, its wheels had ten spokes, front and rear, as in the case of some of George's later huts that I have researched.

4. Oval

John Farris's great grandson showed me an original Farris picture which included one of his great grandfather's shepherds' houses that displayed a large oval name plate above the door. Although the writing on the plate was not eligible, we concluded from its size and shape that it looked similar to an oval John Farris & Sons of Shaftesbury name plate (as shown on page 120). The wooden end boards above the door on Farris huts are about 10" deep. Measurements of the plate shown is 12 1/2" x 7 1/2" deep and is included as a good example of the shape only, not the exact size or actual wording.

When snippets of information such as this comes from a member of the J. Farris family, I take things in earnest, and my curiosity starts to grow.

Future discoveries of unrestored John Farris (& Sons) shepherds' huts may eventually provide more clues and evidence of other styles of name plates being used, especially as such a wide range of castings were made at their foundry.

The name plates that I have researched appear to be the original ones on the John Farris huts that I have seen. It's very important to access details carefully where new discoveries are apparent, as with such a diverse range of castings, it would be easy for one to find its way onto a John Farris hut restoration project causing confusion for enthusiasts of the future. Certainly, unrestored huts are preferable when trying to collate evidence, although they are becoming increasingly difficult to find.

It is apparent, however, that the type of name plate, and specific characteristics of a hut, such as the type of axles and wheels, interior roof supports (e.g. iron or wood), and the detailing of general ironwork and fittings, may give clues to an approximate year of manufacture (e.g late 19th or early 20th century) and can be helpful in identifying whether its possibly an example made by George or John. There will always be a number of inconsistencies between some examples researched, especially when they have been restored, had different name plates attached, or perhaps been altered and modified over the years, such as replacement wheels, axles and ironwork.

The difficulties in accurately identifying some huts without a name plate can easily lead to incorrect presumptions, so it's worth doing ones research carefully.

For example, an interesting hut that I have seen was a small shepherd's house (approx. 10ft x 6ft) with a missing name plate that had similarities to a J. Farris model. Wheels were of the Farris thin spoked type (e.g. front 25" with eight spokes, rear 35" with ten spokes). The chassis consisted of five main beams, but both the chassis and body had been shortened slightly, possibly due to rotten chassis timber joints. The thickness of the chassis was 3" x 3 1/2" deep.

The interior resembled a J. Farris hut and had a curved wrought iron roof support and small window that slid to the rear. Floorboards and internal panelling both measured 5 1/2" wide. The top front wooden axle beam was original, and in a very fragile condition, but had the familiar front axle side support braces and correct style turntable. The lower front wooden beam and rear wooden axle were replacements and modifications to the general axle ironwork seemed apparent.

First impressions are that there are certainly similarities to a J. Farris hut, with many 'boxes being ticked' to this affect. However, although there is a good possibility that it could be one of John's huts, it's important not to presume it's definitely one without further detailed research, measurements and comparisons being carried out. Ideally, this could be compared with another similar example of the same size, with original name plate attached, in order to help accurately ascertain its authenticity as a genuine J. Farris construction.

Farris name plates are always situated outside on the timber apex end boards, centrally above the door. George Farris examples that I have seen are attached with two screws onto these timber boards. It is advisable to consider replacing these screws with small coach bolts, washers and nuts, to deter anyone from easily removing them without permission, as they are becoming collectable in their own right. The early John Farris circular and horseshoe name plates had three screw holes, to secure them. The later John Farris & Sons rectangular and large oval castings had two screw holes.

It is worth checking the original end boards (if still present) above the door as they can give valuable clues as to the correct size of the original name plate if missing. For example, a slight change in colour or an impression on the boards where the name was displayed will help determine the shape, and signs of drilled holes (measure the distance between them) will help to provide an idea of the overall size. It's also useful to take photos for reference purposes.

John Farris Huts

The following photo's show a selection of John's huts that were made at the Shaftesbury Works.

Circular name plate (J. Farris)

A late 19th century John Farris shepherd's hut dating from around the late 1880's displaying a circular name plate with wooden front axle, iron rear axle & ash horse shafts. This example was included on Channel 4's *Amazing Spaces Programme* in 2013. It also features in the excellent accompanying book on the series.

The professionalism and skill carried out by Eddie Butterfield during its restoration was truly outstanding. His use of a steam engine to power traditional machinery for cutting replacement chassis and axle timbers combined with his blacksmith expertise and experience makes him a unique restorer of these antique huts, which has produced very pleasing results.

This example was included on the Amazing Spaces Programme, on Channel 4, in 2013.

Walking into a 'time warp' is probably the best description that can be given for the interior which has been sympathetically preserved. The original corrugated roof sheeting is unusual, having been laid in a haphazard fashion over horse hair insulation.

This is the shepherd's house made by Sybil's great uncle John that she witnessed being towed by a horse in the chapter 'A Special Event' (page 89).

Size:
11 ft 9" x 6ft (141" long x 73" wide).
Wheels: eight spokes front, ten spokes rear.

Options:
Wooden front & rear axles.
Wooden front & iron rear axles.
Wrought iron front & rear axles.

During restoration.

Horseshoe name plate (J. Farris)

A late 19th century John Farris shepherd's hut of similar age to the circular name plate example, but with wrought iron front and rear axles, and displaying a large horse shoe name plate.

This particular hut required an extensive but sympathetic restoration, and was very original and complete. The main chassis beams were rotten at the rear end and unfortunately required replacing, but the interior was very sound and authentic without any signs of rat damage to the floor or matchboarding.

Without doubt, an excellent and rare survivor of a J. Farris shepherd's hut that deserved a sensitive and careful approach to its restoration, due to many of its original features and detailing being present.

Size: 11ft x 7" x 6ft (139" long x 72" wide).
Wheels: eight spokes front, ten spokes rear.

Small rectangular name plate (J. Farris & Sons)

The shepherd's house researched was thought to be quite a late hut, probably dating from around the early 1920's. It displayed a small rectangular name plate including the word 'Sons' on it. Its wooden front and rear axles and corrugated roof sheets had been renewed, but its wonderful aged interior, although a little nibbled around the edges, had a tremendous amount of early jottings on the panelling including evidence of a 1920's date.

Size: approx. 12ft x 6ft.
Wheels: ten spokes front & rear.

A Glimpse

A glimpse of the buttercups through the tiny window,
The ray of light flickering through the open door,
A hint of a draught on the summer breeze,
Shadows creeping across the wooden pine floor.

A glimpse of dust settling on the broken furniture,
Spiders busily spinning their webs all day long,
A mouse being eaten by wriggling maggots,
The woodworm are dead now, and have gone.

A glimpse of some rusty tin flapping in the wind,
The bodywork creaking when moving inside,
Its wheels have seen better days over the years,
In the past, they would have given a good ride.

A glimpse of where a stove had once been,
The flue removed, the rain now leaks in,
Signs of decaying in the rear floorboards,
Restoration work urgently needs to begin.

A glimpse of hope for this poor wreck,
Sympathetically restore it with loving care,
Somehow it needs to be carefully rescued,
Dug out, removed and spared.

Rollin

A poem inspired by the discovery of
a dilapidated shepherd's hut.

Preserving Huts

Preservation of original shepherds' huts is always preferable, as one is dealing with part of our rural heritage, therefore deserving a sympathetic approach during a restoration in order to maintain their character and originality.

During the 21st century, altering Victorian or Edwardian examples that are still in fairly original and overall sound condition, would in my opinion be a tragedy. Certainly, in the case of Sybil's granary, it would financially be more valuable converted into a traditional shepherd's hut, with window, internal panelling and stove fitted. The temptation to install a period tortoise stove has crossed my mind, as the only modification would be to fit the correct type flue casting onto the roof sheeting to take a 3" flue. This would make it far cosier to use during the winter months as a stove can produce a tremendous amount of heat for such a confined space, as well as providing a facility to boil water for a cup of coffee or tea. However, from a historic point of view, it is more important to preserve it as a granary in order to retain part of our heritage in its original form and glory.

Some genuine huts are discovered and modernised by fitting additional windows, which requires new holes being cut into the original corrugation and interior wooden

J. Farris hut interior.

panelling. I agree that in many cases, adding extra windows can enhance the experience of a lighter and more open space inside as well as creating a very pleasant environment to entertain family and friends in. It can also be easier to sell a hut with a larger window installed, as it seems to have a wider appeal to prospective purchasers. Including unnecessary insulation (especially if a stove is present), electricity, solar panels and various other modifications also significantly affects the overall ethos of a sympathetic restoration.

Modernising part of our heritage in this way feels uncomfortable to me. Perhaps one should consider a new shepherd's hut built to ones own specific requirements in order to preserve the antiquity and specification of an original shepherd's house. It certainly makes sense to me!

There are some excellent new examples made that faithfully follow the simple design of original huts, using traditional materials and methods to reproduce something familiar to what a shepherd may have once used whilst tending his flock. Many incorporate a traditional timber chassis, impressive cast iron wheels, larger windows and a few appealing accessories such as a fitted stove, bed, table, curtain rail and coat hooks, etc.

Numerous shepherds' huts have already had additional or larger windows fitted during their lifetime, and it can rightly be debated that this is part of their history. In this instance, one can enjoy the advantages of more light and a better view and reminiscence on their past, or alternatively restore it back to its original specification.

What I do find refreshing, is that there are some reputable specialists and enthusiasts who do their best to sell unmodified shepherds' houses to customers who want to keep them as original as possible. This has to be a good thing for enthusiasts in a climate of quick 'make overs' and trendy fashion statements. By no means is this a criticism of people wanting to decorate their 'pride and joy' with soft furnishings and making them more comfortable (my wife would have it no other way!) but more of a sigh of relief that some sellers and new owners are taking responsibility for a small piece of British history that has become very fashionable in recent years.

A good example can be seen with historic buildings, where it wasn't that many years ago when people were ripping out beautiful Victorian features such as fireplaces, cast iron baths, doors and windows, and modernising everything beyond recognition. Many of today's purchasers now crave for originality and character, and are prepared to pay a premium for them.

Often original doors have also been replaced over the years, sometimes with a window installed in the top section, which can look in keeping and does provide another source of natural light. On the rare occasion where a genuine Farris door (usually without a window) is present, it's encouraging to see it preserved in its original form.

Old and neglected huts often require replacement wooden axles, repairs to wheels, chassis members, floors, doors, windows, and corrugated sheeting, including the roofs. It's important, however, to remember to be very sympathetic with restoration projects, and concentrate on original detailing which will contribute in retaining its authenticity, character and overall historic ambience. A continuing emphasis throughout this book!

Nevertheless, there are occasions when timbers will need replacing if they are rotten. The timber chassis and wooden axles are perhaps areas where renewal is sometimes essential due to their poor and fragile state. It is crucial that a wooden chassis is in reasonably sound condition, and although it may be possible to repair some sections, one needs to access its durability to avoid expensive problems occurring in the foreseeable future.

It is always best to use nuts, bolts, nails and screws similar to the originals, if the old ones are found to be damaged and not reusable. For example, wood screws with slotted heads are desirable as modern screws with crossed heads look totally wrong. There may need to be a compromise with brass or plated screws, although this isn't ideal. Sometimes a good supply of old stock may become available. Number 12 x

1 1/2" screws are always a useful size, especially when attaching door hinges. Replacement ironwork such as bolts for the axles and floor nails should be handmade by a blacksmith to the genuine pattern.

A good quality wood treatment to eradicate and prevent woodworm and wood rot is in many cases essential, in order to help preserve both new and existing timbers. Using a clear wood treatment is usually advisable, particularly with the interior, although a light coloured preservative can look good on the axles.

G. Farris shepherd's hut.

Ideally, avoid sand papering the interior, as this will remove any original patina or jottings, and think carefully before deciding to paint inside a hut. Remember, preservation is always more important than a quick makeover. If previously painted, still act with caution and care and continue a sympathetic approach with your decisions of how to proceed with a restoration.

A traditional dye such as Van Dyke crystals is good to blend in colours of new and old wood, but can be hard to find these days. If using this type of water based dye, it may not be suitable for exterior woodwork as the colour can fade in time. Caution needs to be taken when using some modern dyes, stains and varnishes, as they have a tendency to make a hut look too modern or over restored.

A preserved message from a shepherd.

A clear bee's wax to seal the interior wood panelling and floor, as well as various ironwork, such as the door catch, will all help to achieve an excellent traditional finish. Personally, I find bees wax looks perfect on the exterior of a hut door to enhance the appearance of the wood, but unfortunately needs reapplying too regularly. Oil products such as Danish oil or linseed oil are generally better options for protection against the weather. Very successful results can be achieved by applying Van Dyke solution to help colour-tone a carefully prepared door and then finishing off with one of these oils. I tend to reapply oil about once a year to help maintain the wood against the elements. Alternatively, the doors can be gloss painted, using an appropriate primer and undercoat.

A light oil or wax is excellent for preserving forged ironwork which is not handled very often, such as iron axles and drawbars. I try to avoid using modern gloss paints on such items as it tends to make a restoration look too new. A rusty finish also looks in keeping which can have a light oil or wax applied if required. However, paints do mellow with age, and whatever products are used in a restoration, use them with careful consideration in order to retain some of the historical significance that one should endeavour to achieve.

Where stoves and flues are present, always use a black stove paste to blacken in the traditional way as heat resistant paints look far too modern, and in some instances can eventually blister and peel where the surface is not too sound.

Fitting a traditional stove is usually fairly straight forward. Where the flue passes through the original casting on the roof, a heat resistant rope is used to help position the flue centrally, and a heat resistant sealant is then used to make everything water proof. If in doubt, and where a hut has not previously had a stove, ask a specialist for advice and help, as health and safety in this area is paramount.

If installing an old stove and flue oneself, it's useful to have some assistance at hand inside the hut when one's outside on a ladder, precariously leaning against the roof and sorting out any installation requirements. It doesn't take much movement for the end of the flue to slip out of the rear of a stove, resulting in the flue disappearing through ones hands at an alarming rate and smashing everything in its way as it crashes to the floor inside. Such experiences are not for the faint hearted!

Making a metal flue cap is also important, if an original cast cap is unavailable, to help prevent rain from running down the flue and seeping into the stove. Periodic use of stoves is recommended to keep them dry and moisture out!

Stoves are a main feature, so it is well worth the time and trouble to achieve a good finish. I use a wire brush to remove the surface rust and then apply a rust treatment, and when dry, use a traditional graphite paste on both stove and flue. The exposed part of the flue that sticks out of the roof, will in time, eventually start to appear rusty, but this looks far more in keeping than a modern heat resistant paint.

Tortoise stoves that have rust holes in the thin metal outer 'liner' should be professionally repaired, and not botched with filler, as is often the case. A competent blacksmith can make a new liner and rivet it into position as it was originally made. Alternatively, nuts and bolts could be used to secure the liner. The stove base and fire bricks can be repaired or replaced as necessary. There is a professional product on the market that can be mixed and used instead of old fire bricks, and is excellent for repairing cracked bases, in accordance with the manufacturers instructions. However, it's essential to ensure the stove is restored and fitted to a very high standard for obvious health and safety reasons, so if in doubt, it's prudent to have it professionally repaired and fitted by a competent and recommended specialist. It's also important to always ensure there is adequate ventilation provided in such a confined space when a stove is in use. This may seem obvious but can easily be overlooked with potentially tragic circumstances occurring.

Painting the interior panelling is an option, as long as there are no old internal jottings or markings, although my personal preference is towards retaining originality, character and age, rather than making original interiors look too modern. Windows can also create challenges, as gloss paints can make window frames look too bright, and some stains look too new or dark. A certain amount of experimentation is usually required to achieve acceptable results.

Painting the corrugated sheeting with a good quality paint is a good idea to help preserve it, as well as for aesthetic reasons, although the purist may prefer to leave the corrugation in an 'as found condition', if still serviceable. It's also worth considering sealing the corrugated roof with a couple of coats of a bitumen based product to avoid water seeping in, and in many cases may prove essential.

Restoration projects often show the remains of tar, pitch or bitumen on the roof and side panelling and in some unfortunate cases, tar mixed with sand.

Painted interior with new fittings.

Corrugated sheeting on genuine huts will always look battered, with rust holes, pitting and denting being the norm, and even parts of the sheeting being patched to keep the hut watertight. An assessment needs to be made as to the durability of any sheeting in very poor condition, and whether it's worth replacing. It's best to replace any corrugation with a good second hand sheet, if available, which will blend with existing ones.

When inspecting corrugated sheeting, tell tale signs that some may have already been replaced are as follows:

1. New sheets are smooth without any rust pitting, holes or dents.
2. Old sheets may have 'nail locating holes' that don't correspond with the original hut sheets.
3. Modern type sheeting nails have been used to secure replacement sheets.
4. Different shades of colour may determine alternative sheeting has been used.
5. A replacement sheet may have been slid under the existing corrugation as a temporary repair.
6. Modern square section sheeting may have been used to replace the original rounded corrugation (it can happen!).
7. A different width corrugated sheeting may have been used (e.g. Taskers' huts have a wider pitch than standard).

Ideally, only replace any corrugation if essential, as original sheeting that looks worse for wear may be perfectly acceptable as long as it is watertight and performing the job it was intended for, and it's essential to retain as much of the original as possible.

Many huts, including the granary, had the standard size width of corrugation of 3" between the pitch. The company Tasker's were notably different with 5 1/4" width between the pitch.

The remains of what appears to be a J. Farris shepherd's hut awaiting restoration.

Corrugated sheeting was commonly fitted with the edge of one sheet overlapping the sheet next to it, in an orderly manner, and then secured with 'roofing nails'. It has been found, on a very old original John Farris roof, with horse hair insulation, of a more haphazard approach, where the sheets appear to have been originally laid at random and in no apparent logical order. This particular example (e.g. circular name plate) had been used in later life as a grain store and is thought to have spent a lot of time under cover, such as a barn, hence the remarkable survival of its original corrugated sheeting.

The constant air flow between the side galvanised corrugated sheeting and wooden interior panelling has been a blessing in disguise for many huts over the years, as it has helped to preserve the timber. This would probably not have been appreciated by shepherds who had to contend with the draughts in very harsh and cold conditions whilst attending their flock of sheep during lambing time. However, it's very doubtful if many of the interiors would have survived if insulation had been added in between the side panelling, as pockets of dampness would have inevitably seeped in over the years, causing havoc to both the wooden panelling and framework.

Farris did not fit skirting boards to the interior of their shepherds' houses. Some examples are restored with modern skirting boards included to hide defects on the bottom of the internal panelling and floor edges, which has a tendency to look too new. Some imperfections around the panelling and floor edges are to be expected and can be perfectly acceptable, and it could be argued, actually adds character.

An unusual hut survivor requiring restoration (not Farris).

From a historic perspective, there will be the satisfaction that a genuine hut which has been carefully restored and preserved as close as possible to its original design and specification can be enjoyed in its simplest form. A warm stove and candle light has to be experienced when relaxing inside with family and friends, and a good bottle of wine is a bonus.

As the supply of historic huts diminishes, the charm of well restored, sympathetically maintained and unmodified examples will undoubtedly demand a premium price to the collector and enthusiast of the future.

131

*Shepherd relaxing
with his pipe.*

Evidence of the past

Probably one of the best ways of discovering evidence of the past is by looking at unrestored or derelict shepherds' huts that have not been altered too much over the years. This is obviously becoming more difficult as original ones are increasingly harder to find, and examples that are discovered and appear for sale are usually 'snapped up' to be restored by an enthusiast or specialist.

The interior was fairly basic, with a single bed, table, medicine cupboard and stove sometimes included into the design of some makes of huts, although they were usually optional. These items are normally missing in huts requiring restoration but close examination of the interior can sometimes provide clues to their existence.

Finding and including small period furniture and fittings is always an enjoyable experience, but ideally it's better to display free standing furniture to avoid drilling into the original panelling. It is certainly not beyond the means of a practical person to build a wooden freestanding double bed that slides back into a single bed (or bench), and looks in keeping with the overall period decoration. A small Victorian table and a couple of chairs will help set the scene.

There appears little evidence that either of the Farris brothers included much more than an optional stove in their hut interiors. Markings on the wooden floor, or galvanised sheeting that was sometimes placed under or behind the stove, complete with a hole in the roof for the flue, is all that can usually be found in unrestored examples. Every so often, it is possible to identify lighter marks on the wooden panels surrounding a stove as evidence of ribbed corrugation having been previously fitted.

Perhaps a piece of timber attached to the side of the interior panelling, or a few screw holes may hint of a folding table or bed being included at some time over the years. Certainly, Farris huts may be discovered on the odd occasion with a bed and lambing crib in them, but these items could have been added at a later date.

It is possible that in some instances, employers may have provided their shepherds with some basic freestanding furniture, such as bed, chair or stool, table and small trunk to store some tools or medicines for his sheep and lambs.

Sybil remembers her Uncle Jim having a bunk bed made for his Farris hut positioned across the

From Young Farmers booklet No.16 (1945).

An unrestored gem of an interior.

Evidence of a cricket fan. 1926 Ashes winning England Captain Percy Chapman.

A record of the Bladen Estate 'Big Push' 1932 (shoot?).

forward end, but did not recall her grandfather's business ever making furniture for customers.

Other manufacturers huts can sometimes show evidence of beds that included a secure area underneath for new born lambs to sleep, with the addition of slats, or round doweling, incorporated to provide security for them. A little hinged door could also be added. Sometimes a small table was attached to the panelling below the window and designed to hinge downwards when not in use, and a wooden medicine cabinet may have been placed above the shepherd's bed.

Telltale signs of a shepherd's residents can now and then be seen on the inside wooden panelling, such as numbers of sheep counted, reference to the weather, messages or notes to the farmer, branding iron marks and splashes of ruddle dye (or chalk) used for marking the sheep. Old nails and hooks, and even bits of old newspaper dated around the turn of the century and used to block out draughts, and autographs scribbled in pencil by previous occupiers, all add interest and provide evidence of times gone by.

A few huts were used by prisoners of war and the home guard, and jottings on the interior panellings can sometimes be discovered in a foreign language and provides interesting reading, and are always worth preserving.

One unrestored hut that I was invited to examine had sketches of faces drawn on the interior panelling, which were remarkably good, both in artistic talent as well as overall condition. Owned by a very knowledgeable and helpful shepherd's hut enthusiast and specialist who is still restoring and making shepherds' houses in his family business at Sixpenny Handley in the Wiltshire area.

Granary evidence

The inside of Sybil's granary displays a surprising amount of historical jottings considering it lacks any internal wooden panelling, and was not used as a shepherd's house. The majority are found on the exposed timber frame, but also on the corrugated sheeting.

Some of the jottings are faint scribbles, and are not easily decipherable. The name 'Ernest Fry' is however very neatly and clearly written onto the timber (e.g. offside near the front, just below the roof line) and is understood to be one of the craftsmen of George Farris who built the granary. The name was concealed by an 8ft cane that was resting on some nails. The name 'S. Fry' is also evident in a few places, and the initials 'EF' are also imprinted into the timber. Angela says that 'the last Fry died in the village a couple of years ago'.

It is just possible to make out the name and location of 'L. Harper, Shrewton, Wilts', which is neatly pencilled into the framework. Shrewton is near Stonehenge, which is fairly close to Salisbury and Coombe Bissett.

Another old and faded jotting shows 'Spade & ????? 28/2/07', deciphered as 28 Feb 1907 or possibly 01? as joined up writing, which is particularly interesting and important because of the date. This certainly provides some evidence that Sybil's granary was in use during the Edwardian period.

The exact year the granary was built is unclear, but with some unusual construction detailing, including a hessian internal lining, and evidence of a date, suggests it is at least Edwardian and could possibly be late Victorian. Certainly, Sybil and her daughter Angela surmised it could be late Victorian as it has the early type name plate with a 'G', as well as a few unusual and early features, and they included family ages and dates in their overall assessment.

There are quite a few other markings inside Sybil's granary, some no doubt later additions as they are roughly gouged into the wood (e.g. HS, TS, WR), and others pencilled and too difficult to read.

With a little time studying scribbles closely, and applying white chalk to the faint lettering, I have found that it is sometimes possible to make more sense of them. One such example was in a Lott & Walne hut, where by applying chalk to some light impressions left by a pencil on the internal panelling, the words 'BCK 3rd DEC', abbreviated for Back 3rd Dec, and presumably a message to the farmer left by the shepherd, became a lot clearer. Alternatively, photographing faint scribbles can also provide some surprising results.

As previously mentioned, during a conversation with Sybil, I had been told that George used to collect the corrugated sheeting for the shepherds' huts from Salisbury railway station. Evidence is provided on the rear internal roof of the granary (door side) where the corrugation has a 'delivery note' written on it stating '21 (presumably the number of sheets delivered) Salisbury Stn, C/o Hooper & Ashby, Salisbury'. The name and address are also evident on one of the side sheets (e.g. near the rear, offside) and also on the front nearside roof sheet.

The late George Farris head carpenter, John Judd, celebrated his 100th birthday in 2008, and had lived in Coombe Bissett for the majority of his life. It would certainly be fascinating to discover his name or initials in one of George's huts.

Other eventual uses of shepherds' houses were as grain stores, temporary animal and chicken shelters, gamekeepers accommodation and store, and even for point to point horse racing shelters. An example used for this latter purpose has a window running along the full length of the hut and was used by point to point officials for years. It is now owned by a shepherd's hut specialist and enthusiast near Stroud. An important part of its history, and

perhaps a good case for leaving it in this altered form. In more recent years, this interesting shepherd's hut appeared in one of the Nanny McPhee films.

Old photographs and pictures are another important source that provides evidence of the past. A useful example already mentioned was one with J. Farris & Sons workers standing behind a banner, which provided important details during the research and reconstruction of some new horse shafts.

Sybil's old photograph of an unusual George Farris shepherd's hut standing in front of the Coombe Bissett Steam Plough Works with a rectangular name plate and its traditional Farris spoked wheels is also an important find. This unusual hut has the door at the 'horse shaft end' and a large window either side of the bodywork.

Apart from showing an unusual hut in front of the original building, one is just able to identify part of a 'see saw' plough, and the outline of another shepherd's hut in the background.

Once in a while, old catalogues are also discovered which include shepherds' houses, although these are becoming harder to find. One surprising example was in a 1929 Harrods catalogue, of Brompton Road, London. In their Ironmongery department they advertised a small portable iron shepherd's hut (10ft long x 6ft wide) with matchboard interior, boarded floor and very small wheels, therefore requiring no steps. Hut price £16. 18. 9 (carriage paid). Stove & pipe £1.16. 3 extra. Shafts & fore-carriage £6. 3. 0 extra.

PORTABLE IRON SHEPHERD'S HUT.

No. I R 460.

Framed of Round Timber, covered outside with Galvanised Corrugated Iron, lined inside with matchboarding, boarded floor, mounted on strong wheels and axles, double doors as shown.

Size, 10 ft. long, 6 ft. wide, 6 ft. high to eaves.   Price £16 18 9 Carriage Paid.

Stove and Pipe £1 16 3 extra.   Tubular Shafts and Forecarriage £6 5 0 extra.

Similar shaped huts were also made by Boulton & Paul of Norwich, and R. Mallon of Norfolk. A picture in this book (pages 138 & 157) of a 'decaying hut languishing in a cherry orchard' is a good example of this styling and construction, and although not made by Farris, is an excellent example of what can still be discovered when taking a stroll in the countryside.

Rare antique auctioneers catalogues and posters are also fascinating to read. For example, Messrs. Wyatt & Son produced farming stock catalogues for their auctions (e.g. Marden, Sussex Sales, 1891 & 1893) where shepherds' houses, on four wheels, were advertised. Such catalogues provide historic evidence of second hand shepherds' houses from estates of people who had died or perhaps retired, being sold and bought during the 19th century, as an alternative to buying new. These particular examples are interesting as the location of the auctions were in the heart of the South Downs, an area where many shepherds' huts were being used during lambing time.

Sybil mentioned in her article that George Farris used a donkey drawn wheelchair during his latter years due to rheumatoid arthritis, as transport around the Coombe Bissett premises. During one of our conversations she also commented that 'his donkey was kept at the rear of his cottage, near the back door'. Snippets of information such as this from George's granddaughter can conjure up all sorts of images in ones mind of

Donkey Shoe.

how he coped on a day to day basis with the running of his business whilst suffering from health problems, and how important his donkey was in order to provide mobility for him around the foundry. Sybil kindly gave me one of George's donkey shoes to display in her old granary.

Early photographed cards, adverts and prints are worth studying and are becoming very collectable. They can at times show shepherds with some of their tools of the trade, such as crooks, lanterns, bells, costrels, bags, sacks, hurdles and dogs. Many include scenes of sheep grazing and sheep being dipped, as well as the countryside and farming in general. Early period clothing (e.g. worn by shepherds) can also be examined from these pictures.

Photo card c.1900, Shepherd (thought to be Charles Trigwell), dog & sheep.

Old post cards and antique prints also give a valuable insight into local period architecture including churches, houses and pretty thatched cottages. Roads and bridges may include a pony and trap, sheep being 'drove' along a road, or possibly a field with an agricultural implement being used.

There are also some very good books which include stories and information on 19th century shepherds which are worth sourcing. Some early editions that are out of print are becoming very collectable, but are usually expensive and can be incredibly hard to find. My personal favourites are by authors such as Barclay Wills, W. H. Hudson and A. L. J. Gossett, which are essential reading for anyone interested in shepherding from bygone days.

Period pictures and adverts of shepherds' huts are also increasingly difficult to discover, but I always live in hope!

If unable to visit places like Coombe Bissett, Tollard Royal and Shaftesbury, then studying old post cards, prints, photographs, maps or early local history books on these areas are essential if one wants to experience the atmosphere of when these Farris huts were made and used on the downs and surrounding countryside during the end of the 19th century.

Shaftesbury features in some of Thomas Hardy's novels (renamed as Shaston) such as *Jude the Obscure*. Hardy referred to Shaftesbury as 'the city of dream', and is certainly worth a visit.

Living with the dead

Wonder what might have been,
Snuggled up and so warm,
The bed is too cramped!
But still sleep till dawn.

The memories of the past,
So blatant yet obscure,
Reminder of yesteryear,
Feeling evermore pure.

The hardship and tears,
Lavished so readily and free,
To tender the heart
With a fond memory.

Minds of distinction
Can roam and distress,
Confusion and imaginary,
A form of progress.

Forever in one's thoughts,
The shadows of despair,
A glimmer of hope
That kindness is there.

The comfort of good feelings,
What might have been said,
The mind playing games,
Living with the dead.

Rollin

Whilst thinking about previous life in my J. Farris shepherd's hut, 'Living With The Dead' just came from nowhere! It's a little dark, but a particular favourite of mine.

John Farris (& Sons)

A brief overview.

John Farris was the elder brother of George Farris, who, without the tragedy of the shooting accident in 1882, would probably have continued working and living next to his younger brother at Coombe Bissett, and expanded the business together, as their eldest brother Charles had envisaged before his fatal riding accident. This was not to be, and John moved to manage the Tollard Royal (Homington) and Shaftesbury foundries sometime after this date.

I have no evidence to suggest that huts had ever been built at the Tollard Royal foundry, and having spoken to Sybil about this, it appears unlikely. It is also unclear exactly when John started building shepherds' huts at Shaftesbury, although it is thought to be sometime during the late 1880's.

Certainly, by the early 1890's John Farris was living with his wife Ellen and children, Charles, William, Emily, John and Rose, at Semley Road, Shaftesbury. The 1891 Census, Shaftesbury Holy Trinity, confirms this, and lists him as a 46 year old and an implement maker in agriculture at the Tollard Royal foundry, Wiltshire.

Gold Hill, Shaftesbury.

John's two eldest children, Charles, aged 19, and William, aged 17, we're also classified as implement makers in agriculture, but were apparently at the time of the census in New York, USA. The classification 'implement makers' suggests the possibility that they could have been involved in their father's business before travelling to the U.S.A.

John had started building shepherds' houses before his sons joined him and continued production later on with their help. His earlier shepherds' huts displayed name plates J. Farris, with later ones J. Farris & Sons. The address on the plates were Belle Vue Works, Shaftesbury, or just Shaftesbury. Note the location of the address!

An observation of the 1895 Kelly Directory shows that John was an agricultural implement maker, but was now registered at the Belle Vue Works in Shaftesbury (not Tollard Royal).

Interestingly, there is reference in a 1895 Exhibition Catalogue published by Pitt Rivers of a model traction engine, that was made and exhibited at the famous Larmer Tree Pleasure Grounds, by Messrs. J. Farris & Sons, of Shaftesbury. These are the same grounds that Sybil mentioned in her article on the Coombe Bissett Steam Plough Works, and were created by General Pitt Rivers during the late 19th

A fine display of John Farris artifacts, featuring a Charles Farris model engine.

century. Reference to this 1895 Exhibition Catalogue is an important date, as it refers to J. Farris & Sons, thereby providing evidence that at least two sons (e.g. Charles and William) were definitely working in the business by then.

A model traction engine is regularly displayed at The Great Dorset Steam Fair by a great grandson of John Farris. His grandfather Charles (John Farris's eldest son) built this engine and it is very impressive indeed.

A smaller model traction engine was designed by William Farris (1875 to 1942) and named 'Kitty'. In 1899 William (now 26) married Kate Lovanna in the Parish of Shaftesbury, St James. Tragically, his wife died four years later, so William dedicated the model engine to the memory of his wife. It was displayed at the time in the engineers offices in Victoria Street, Shaftesbury, but is now exhibited in The Gold Hill Museum, situated close to the famous cobbled and picturesque Gold Hill, Shaftesbury.

During the turn of the 19th and 20th centuries, in an area of Shaftesbury known as the Commons (just off the high street), market day regularly saw John Farris & Sons displaying and selling their agricultural machinery and implements. They were also agents for companies such as Amanco, selling stationery engines to run items such as their saw benches and root pulpers. They also specialised in the repair of all types of agricultural machinery, threshing machines and steam rollers.

As discussed earlier, John Farris's shepherds' houses seem to have displayed a relatively small number of cast iron name plates over the years, although evidence of other plates may become available as future unrestored huts are discovered. The company, however, actually had a huge range of name plates attached to other agricultural implements (usually secured with forged nuts and bolts or riveted to the items), as well as their name (and address) included on their castings during the manufacturing process. Some wrought ironwork on their earlier huts can also occasionally be found with the name Farris stamped into them.

Brass name plates were also used on some implements and machinery. I have seen advertised a J. Farris brass plate (size 5" x 3" x 1/4" thick) with 'J Farris, Agent, Belle Vue Iron Works, Shaftsbury'. The letter 'E' was omitted from the name Shaftesbury which is very unusual. Whether this plate was a genuine 19th century example is unclear, although a possibility. A slightly

An excellent display of J. Farris name plates & implement seat.

more elaborate style of lettering than normal and the omission of the 'E' appears inconsistent to John's usual early name plates of the same period. Exceptions can exist, but one should act with caution when accessing their authenticity, especially if making a purchase at an inflated price.

Original 19th century cast iron J. Farris name plates usually have similar style lettering (in capitals) and include the letter 'E' in Shaftesbury, and this is also the case with all the J. Farris & Sons examples that I have examined. It's worth noting that Shaftesbury in Dorset includes an 'E', whereas the spelling of Shaftsbury (without the E) appears more usual in the USA.

Although John Farris shepherds' houses had some similarities to George Farris huts, many of the subtle differences are mentioned in the comparisons discussed in

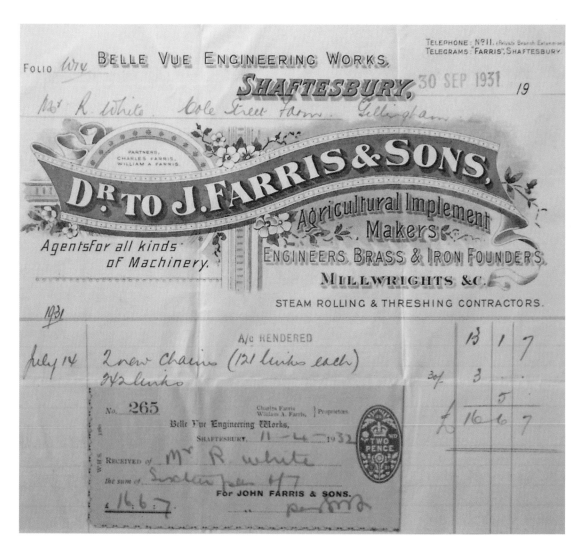

*An original J. Farris & Sons
invoice, dated 1931.*

the chapter on the construction of
Sybil's granary. The most obvious
difference however, is the notably
predominant use of iron axles,
whereas his brother George
preferred using wooden axle
beams. John Farris shepherds'
huts are rarer than George's, but
both are becoming increasingly
harder to find and are highly
sought after by enthusiasts. As far
as individual collectibles are
concerned, George Farris items are
harder to discover, not surprising

John Farris & Sons saw bench.

when one considers the wide range of castings and implements that were made at the Shaftesbury foundry over the years.

It has previously been suggested to me that John Farris & Sons may have used a distribution agent such as Pond & Son (Engineers of Blandford) to sell some of their huts. Having discussed this with a member of the Farris family, we could only surmise as to whether their business might have been too close to the John Farris foundry in Shaftesbury to have made it worth while. There are definite similarities with a Pond & Son hut that I have seen, but further evidence is necessary in order to help clarify this during my on going research. At present, I can only speculate as to whether Pond & Son could possibly have sold huts on behalf of John Farris & Sons. My investigation continues!

John Farris died in 1914. His obituary states he was a member of the local Lodge of Freemasons and a member of the Town Council. He died at Weymouth aged 71 years. His remains were returned to Holy Trinity churchyard in Shaftesbury for interment.

SHAFTESBURY.

DEATH OF MR. J. FARRIS,—Mr. John Farris, the head of the Belle Vue Ironworks, died at Weymouth on Saturday, and the remains having been brought to his home, the interment took place at Holy Trinity churchyard on Wednesday. The Rev. F. Ehlvers conducted the service, which was attended by a very large number of friends and acquaintances. The Mayor and Corporation and the officers of the Council were present in their official capacity, as were the members of the local lodge of Freemasons. Mr. Farris was a member of the Town Council, but was debarred, owing to physical infirmity, from taking an active part in the business of the Council. He was highly respected by a large circle. He was 71 years of age, and leaves a widow and three sons and two daughters.

John Farris & Sons were still trading at the Belle Vue Works in Shaftesbury until the mid 1970's. In 1975, John Farris & Sons sadly ceased trading. This was later confirmed in The London Gazette, 2nd September, 1976, which stated that John Farris & Sons Ltd, Agricultural Engineers, Registered Office; Belle Vue Engineering Works, Shaftesbury, Dorset, went into liquidation.

Competitors of Farris

Recognising manufacturers shepherds' huts is useful when considering purchasing and restoring one. Often name plates are missing, or so worn by the elements that they are indistinguishable, and some companies may not have included their name on their huts at all.

The following information provides the enthusiast with a brief insight of a few of George's competitors during the end of the 19th and early 20th centuries. Many other huts would have been made 'in house' by local farming estates, and these have not been included as they are usually 'one offs' and too diverse for this book. Some of these were made for shepherds to use, complete with interior panelling and stove, whist others were more basic and designed usually as granaries or general storage. Occasionally, there is evidence of some basic examples showing signs of past inhabitants such as shepherds, although they would have been exceedingly uncomfortable compared to panelled versions.

John Farris was certainly one of George's most notable competitors, as it was his brother whom he had fallen out with over very tragic circumstances. There were, however, some other very good firms that produced some excellent shepherds' houses at competitive prices, and a few of my favourite are briefly included below.

Watson & Haig of Andover, Hants

Trading from Acre Iron Works, Andover, Hants, Watson & Haig, agricultural engineers, built their shepherds' houses during the late 19th and early 20th centuries along traditional lines, with wooden chassis and frame, and covered with galvanised corrugated iron, and strong wooden axles and large impressive wheels which are sometimes found to be painted in pitch. Wheels had eight spokes, front and rear. Stub axle end caps are similar in design to Tasker & Sons, but smaller overall.

The sides and ends were lined with matchboarding, whilst lining the roof was an optional extra. Stable doors were fitted to the rear offside of the hut and included a small window, latch and lock. An opening ventilator was fitted into the front wooden apex boards (instead of a small front window), and wooden steps were included. As huts were horse drawn, strong wooden shafts were provided.

Two sizes of portable houses were built.

The larger hut was 12 1/2 ft long x 6 1/2 ft wide, and according to period adverts, cost in the region of £42.00, including stove and flue. Customers would have to pay an extra £2.00 to line the roof with matchboard.

The smaller hut was 10ft long x 5ft wide, and consisted of a lighter frame and wheels. It was probably designed for use as a granary in its basic form, as it had no matchboard lining or stove, and was considerably cheaper at around £27.00. However, lining the sides and ends and the fitting of a stove could be included at an additional cost.

Corrugation was of the standard size (e.g. 3" in between the pitch), and there were spacer blocks (2 3/4" x 1 1/3") to help secure the corrugated sheeting along the bottom of the hut. It is very easy to confuse these spacer blocks with Taskers' huts which had wider corrugation and larger blocks (top and bottom).

Name plates were standard on all models, and some large unrestored examples that I have seen had a name plate on the front and rear ends. Shepherds' houses by Watson & Haig are increasingly becoming difficult to find, so new discoveries should be carefully restored and preserved.

Interestingly, around the turn of the century, Watson and Haig also built horse drawn water carriers, and reference to stacking elevators and hay sweeps can occasionally be found in 1930's adverts.

Lott & Walne Ltd of Dorchester, Dorset

Trading from around 1899 to the late 1960's, Lott & Walne were described as engineers, iron founders and agricultural implement manufacturers. The foundry was based at Fordington and positioned alongside the River Frome, and consisted of a casting shop and blacksmiths. The original building still exists as apartments and bears the Lott & Walne name. The first owner was John Galpins around the early to mid 1800's, who ran the Galpins Iron foundry on the site.

Their diversity of items manufactured ranged from pumping machinery, drain covers, chaff cutters, wheel 'drag shoes' and pony and horse drawn ploughs, and by the late 1940's implements for tractors. A 1909 catalogue lists that Lott & Walne also manufactured liquid manure and water carts with detachable pumps.

In 1905 plans were drawn up which included all measurements and materials to construct their shepherds' huts. A publicity photograph included an example with 'Lott & Walne Ltd Dorchester' written on the side, and also displayed horse shafts.

Photo J.L.

The external body measurements of this hut would have been about 9 3/4 ft long x 6ft wide. Construction consisted of an exterior galvanised corrugated curved roof and side panels, with the interior consisting of a pine floor and 6 1/2" pine tongue and grooved matchboard panelling on the ceiling and sides. The main outer timber chassis beams on examples measured were 3" x 4" deep, whilst the two inner beams were 2" x 4" deep.

A stove could be installed and evidence from early photographs show stove flues went through the rear offside of the corrugated roof.

One of the most distinguishing features of their attractive huts is that the lower front axle beams and rear axles were made of 1 1/2" square section wrought iron.

Early examples had feather edged wooden ends below the roof apex. The front end had a small wooden opening window and wooden frame. Some later ones had corrugated ends, with a front wooden window frame surround and metal opening window and simple latch.

Another feature was that the top opening of the rear door had an 'offset' window. This was due to the window being inserted against the edge of the wide wooden door panel nearest the hinge, thus given it an offset appearance. There were some variations in design with the door catches and wooden steps supplied as a standard fitting.

Earlier huts can occasionally be found with two brackets on the nearside chassis member for a front and rear brake chain. Later examples usually had one bracket.

Name plates appear not to have been included on their huts. Cast iron or brass plates were however attached to some of their other implements and ironwork. Many castings had the name and location incorporated during the manufacturing process, therefore not requiring a name plate.

Lott & Walne provided fairly straight wooden horse shafts. with a small 'ladder' section nearer the axle end.

R & J Reeves & Sons Ltd of Westbury, Wilts

Reeves were based in the Bratton Iron Works at Westbury, and were a well established firm specialising in making agricultural equipment during the 19th century.

An impressive range of items were made by Reeves, such as seeding machines, horse drawn ploughs and hoe's, liquid manure drills and carts, saw benches, sheep racks, corn and seed drills, chain pumps and portable barrow pumps.

Period c.1900 adverts show that they manufactured shepherds' huts and portable granaries. Three sizes of shepherds' houses were offered, starting at around £29,

Body sizes were:

13ft x 6ft 8" x 7ft 4" high.
11ft 8" x 5ft 8" x 7ft 2" high.
9ft 9" x 5ft 3" x 7ft high.

Their construction looked similar in design to other manufacturers of this period, as they had a corrugated exterior, wooden chassis, floor and interior panelling. Axles were of wrought iron. Wheels were cast iron and had six spokes, front and rear. Open stub axle end caps are positioned against the wheel hubs, and solid metal pins hold the assembly together.

The rear doors on their huts were of the stable type, with the top part of the door incorporating a window. An interesting feature was a ventilator fitted above the door.

Period adverts state that matchboard lining the roof with wood was extra. Beds, additional windows and a stove could also be fitted at extra cost at the time of manufacture. Wooden horse shafts were fitted as standard and a name plate was also included.

Reeves & Sons produced hand drawings for their huts dating from about 1896 onwards, showing construction detailing, such as dimensions, and type of timber and ironwork used.

Interestingly, some of Reeves shepherds' houses have been discovered with John Wallis Titt name plates on them. In 1874 John Titt was registered as an agricultural engineer and iron founder at the Woodcock Ironworks, Warminster, Wiltshire, producing items such as elevators.

He was well known for his wind engines used to pump water, drive farming implements and even produced electricity. The wind engines were the Woodcock, Simplex direct, and the Simplex geared.

Some of John Wallace Titt period catalogues advertised Reeves goods, and his company also acted as a distributing agent selling Reeves shepherds' houses with their own company name on them.

Tasker & Sons, Nr. Andover, Hants

Tasker's were a well established company, based at the Waterloo Foundry, near Andover, Hants, and started to build shepherds' huts around the turn of the 19th to 20th centuries. They also manufactured agricultural implements such as ploughs, harrows, cultivators and elevators.

Their portable houses were 10ft x 5ft 6" and 12ft 6" x 6ft 6" with a cheaper quality option available.

They are instantly distinguishable by their unusually wide ribbed corrugated sheeting and large iron spacer blocks (3" x 2 1/2") running along the bottom (and top) of the corrugated sheeting to help secure them in position. Tasker's used rivets to secure the corrugated sides, corners and roof during their construction. Interestingly, corrugated sheets on their earlier huts were not galvanised.

An opening air vent (sometimes one either end) and name plate were located on the wooden apex boards. The door incorporated a small window and was positioned on the

A Tasker hut awaiting restoration. Note the wider sheeting pitch, riveting and spacer blocks.

rear offside. A stove and flue could be included as an extra, and were positioned inside opposite the doorway.

The wooden interior panelling was also unusual as it ran horizontally, instead of vertically, as in the case of many other makes, including Farris.

Some examples were constructed without windows, but an additional window could be fitted as an extra, and was recommended for keepers use. Axles were wooden. Wheels were heavy duty. Front wheels had six

G. Farris alongside a Tasker & Sons hut.

or eight spokes. Rear wheels eight or nine spokes. Tapered wrought iron stub axles allow for enclosed cast iron caps to be positioned against the wheel hubs. A round solid pin goes through individual caps in order to hold the wheels securely in place.

Restoration can sometimes be a problem when sourcing the wider corrugated sheeting. Replacement of damaged corrugation is also made more difficult due to the riveting that secures it in place. Traditional old pig houses may be a good place to look for second hand roof sheeting. The width of the sheeting is 5 1/4" (in between the pitch).

A rare survivor of a c.1800's shepherd's hut by H. Kendall.

Researching other hut makers

Further research of other hut makers is in progress, and a few are briefly mentioned below:

During one of my conversations with Sybil, she recalled 'another hut maker down the road in Blandford'. This may have been Ingrams & Co, Engineers of Blandford, who apparently also made shepherds huts. Investigations are proceeding with this one!

A recent restoration project by Eddie Butterfield of a rare unrestored hut made by T. H.Kendall of Cashmore, Blandford (c.1880 or earlier, and still with its original name plate attached) is proof of an early hut builder previously located in the Blandford area. The 10ft x 6ft 6" body was predominately made from wood, and four robust cast iron wheels, 32" high x 4 1/2" wide with nine spokes was incorporated into the design. The interior of the example undergoing restoration boasted its original medicine cupboard and genuine bed that hinged upwards against the panelling.

Unrestored interior (H. Kendall).

Mr Kendall senior of Cashmore was the landlord of the local public house. His son was involved with the running of the Implement Works opposite, where they made shepherds' huts.

An original interior,
dated 1891. Photo J.L.

Slightly further afield was a company called Thomas Baker & Sons who were a late Victorian engineering company that was based in Compton, on the Berkshire Downs. Their horse drawn shepherds' houses and portable granaries, approximate sizes 10ft x 6ft and 12ft x 6ft, are uncommon and consisted of a wooden chassis, galvanised corrugated sides and a curved roof, small window, very attractive ironwork and traditional wooden axles with cast iron wheels consisting of six spokes.

A few c.1900 catalogues show that they also made village pumps and agricultural implements, including liquid manure and water carts. Some of their impressive 4ft agricultural implement wheels can be found stamped Baker Compton around the wheel hub area.

Rural scene.
Photo J.L.

Hut Prices

During one of our conversations, Sybil remarked that the cost of buying a new Farris shepherd's hut would have been around the same price as their competitors. although prices would have fluctuated over the years due to factors such as increases in material costs, demand, etc.

Certainly, today's prices can vary quite considerably with historic shepherds' huts, depending on factors such as originality, manufacturer, size, condition, and overall desirability (e.g. name plate, size of wheels, stove, provenance, etc). Larger examples are usually more sought after as they provide additional interior space and are generally more useful for families; a spare bedroom, studio, children's living space, garden room, romantic retreat, or even a 19th century time warp where one can temporarily get away from modern day living and reality. However, all sizes of huts make very attractive features, whether displayed in a garden, meadow, woodland, or even by a pond where their reflections create a whole new dimension to their setting.

Huts with their original name plates are desirable both for authentic reasons as well as providing evidence for research and helping to date them more accurately. Many examples are often thought to be a lot older than they actually are, especially by some of their owners! I have seen a George Farris one advertised as mid Victorian or earlier, which is 'pushing the boundaries', as we know that Sybil's grandfather George (and great uncle John) only moved into the cottages at Coombe Bissett in 1882. Certainly, in the case of Farris, this book does provide useful evidence of when the Farris brothers were trading, and acts as an authoritative guide for the enthusiast to reasonably estimate how old and original their huts could realistically be.

Condition is obviously very important as this can determine both originality as well as potential restoration costs, and is probably one of the most crucial factors to consider. An example that retains its original wheels, general forged ironwork and stove is a huge bonus as finding replacement parts is very time consuming and becoming increasingly difficult to source.

Some people would not even consider buying an original shepherd's house in any condition, and prefer to purchase a bespoke new hut in immaculate condition made to their specific requirements. This is excellent news for enthusiasts preferring genuine examples to restore as they are becoming harder to find. Old huts will always look a little battered on their corrugated sheeting, showing signs of imperfections such as age related scars and woodworm both to the exterior and interior timbers, including floor, axles and chassis members. I find

A fine example of a modern classic by Eddie Butterfield.

Decaying hut languishing in a cherry orchard.

this is what attracts me, as I love the character and history that oozes from them, plus the challenge and excitement of renovating a new discovery.

As a rough guide, expect to pay a few thousand pounds for an unrestored example requiring a complete restoration, particularly if it is made by well known manufacturers such as Farris, Lott & Walne, Reeves and Watson & Haig. Prices for some of the larger original shepherds' houses sympathetically restored, with correct detailing and in excellent condition, with well preserved interior panelling and fitted with original stove, name plate, etc, can easily reach into double figures.

Seasonal factors and current trends can also influence prices, with huts usually realising slightly higher prices during the spring and summer months. Historic huts over the last few years, including wrecks, have generally been increasing in price due to their scarcity, with good and pretty examples usually being snapped up quickly if advertised realistically.

When considering making a purchase, whether privately or through a specialist, it is worth remembering that there could be expensive transport costs involved. This is specifically relevant, where for example, a private sale may have advertised a derelict and unrestored wreck which is fairly inaccessible, such as under brambles, on soft ground or in a remote location. Huts are large and heavy, and recovery in some circumstances can be very difficult, so professional help may be necessary.

Always go and look at a hut before buying it. This may sound obvious, but it is easy to impulse buy, for example through an on line auction, only to find it is not quite in the condition that it was thought to be in. If possible, do some research beforehand and take someone knowledgable with you for advice.

Be aware that a hut might not have been built originally as a shepherd's house, but may have been converted into one at a later date by using, for example, an old farm threshing machine chassis, turntable and cast iron wheels. This may be very acceptable for some enthusiasts if purchased with the knowledge of its past history, and priced accordingly.

It is not uncommon for new owners to think they have purchased an original shepherd's hut by a specific manufacture (e.g. Farris, Watson & Haig, Reeves) when it is obvious to someone with some basic knowledge and experience that its not the genuine thing. A replacement name plate added during a restoration also adds to the confusion, and is becoming more common, so one needs to be careful. For example, an enthusiast at a rally was convinced he had a Lott & Walne example and was looking for an original name plate to attach to it, when in fact his hut appeared to possibly be a rare John Farris survivor.

A few specialists sometimes advertise and sell original examples in 'as found' or restored condition. Prices may be higher than a private sale, but it could be a preferable option, as they have already discovered and recovered the hut, usually have reliable transport arrangements, and often have experience to advise on its authenticity.

It takes time to find an original hut for sale, so some patience when looking is paramount. Searching on the web for adverts and asking specialists is always a good start. 'Word of mouth' from someone who knows you are looking for one is another option, but in my experience is more forthcoming when they see you already own one and enjoy restoring and preserving them. Having a conversation with other enthusiasts may also result in snippets of information about an example requiring some restoration that may possibly be for sale. This is how I discovered Sybil's granary.

If a derelict hut appears to be a rare and desirable restoration project, don't expect information to be that specific or forthcoming.

"Where can I find an original hut" is a question I am often asked. Not always easy to answer if I have my eye on another one at a reasonable price. They can be very addictive and they are becoming more difficult to locate.

It is still possible to sometimes find shepherds' huts and purchase them at affordable prices if found in an unrestored condition. By taking on some of the restoration work oneself, and if carried out over a period of time, projects can become a viable proposition. The biggest problem can often be finding a suitable and attractive specimen and then persuading the owner to sell it to you at a realistic price in order to make the restoration an affordable project. People can become very attached to their huts, and if persuaded to sell, may want quite an inflated price for something that does not appear very restorable. It's important to be sensible with an offer, and with a bit of luck you may eventually be the proud owner of your own piece of history with all the hard work and excitement (including sleepless nights) that a restoration can bring. The reward is your own unique space which can be used throughout the seasons, perhaps as a personal retreat, or for all your family to enjoy.

A room with a view.

Getting closer to nature.

Planning Permission

Generally speaking, planning permission is not usually required when a shepherd's hut is situated in your own garden (or meadow) for your own personal use, as they are a portable agricultural dwelling and therefore not a permanent structure. Nevertheless, restrictions could apply in some circumstances, so it may be prudent to check with your local Planning Office on current planning legislation and any possible local restrictions before purchasing one. This is certainly advisable if you live in a conservation area, decide to change the use of agricultural land to run a business such as a 'Shepherd's Hut Bed & Breakfast' and require electricity and other amenities, or unfortunately have difficult neighbours.

An advantage of historic huts are that they are mobile and can be fairly easily moved around your property to take advantage of a pretty view, a private location, enhance a romantic setting, or even used as it was originally intended during the lambing season. Such diversity of use should always be respected and treasured.

It is also worth ensuring that your hut is covered against fire and theft, and public liability insurance where appropriate.

A space of your own

Inspired whilst relaxing in my shepherd's hut

Crackling of logs on the stove,
Warmth from the heat as they burn,
Smell of the sap as it melts,
A whiff of the smoke on the breeze.

The pattering of feet on the steps,
Creak of the hinge from the door,
The nose that appears from behind
A wet body that flops on the mat.

A tiny space of ones own to enjoy.
To share with family, as and when,
Whether two or four legged, who cares?
Whichever is good company at the time.

A place to imagine and dream,
To float into ones inner self,
Escape for a moment or two,
Feel calm, relaxed and satisfied.

The walls may come alive,
Whispering from the depth of time.
Secrets of the past may haunt you
But they mean you no harm.

Sadness is overcome by joy,
Negatives by many positives,
Mixed emotions, bloody mindedness.
Just move on, don't look behind!

A place to enjoy and be free,
For a moment or two at the most,
Too busy to appreciate very often
It's a space of your own.

Rollin

Brief construction detailing
At a glance

There are instances when researching a hut, where the opportunity may arise to take a few accurate measurements of its construction. If owned by someone else, asking their permission to photograph and study their property is obviously always polite and considerate, and there may be many occasions when it's only possible to admire and observe from a distance, especially if one wants to stay friendly with them.

The brief reference guide below includes some construction detailing of Farris examples that I have been fortunate enough to research, and does provide the enthusiast and restorer with an interesting guide to the subtle differences between some of the Farris models examined for this book. Minor variations in sizes are to be expected between similar examples as they are individually hand built. The availability of materials would also have influenced certain elements of the building process. However, observations and comparisons between George's and John's huts may be helpful when discovering a restoration project (especially with a missing name plate), and helps to provide a useful guide for a reasonable assessment to be made as to its authenticity and originality. All examples of the huts below had their original name plates attached.

Body sizes (external corrugation, approx. sizes).
Note: In brackets: Huts accurately measured in inches.

George Farris - Large Rectangular name plate (very small hut).	8 ft x 6ft
George Farris - Large Rectangular name plate (granary).	10ft x 6ft (122 3/4" x 73 1/2")
George Farris - Large Rectangular name plate (s/hut).	12 ft x 6 1/2 ft (146 1/2" x 74 3/4")
George Farris - Oblong name plate.	12 1/4 ft x 6 1/2 ft (147" x 78")
George Farris - Small Oval name plate.	12 ft x 6 ft 3" (146 1/2" x 75")
John Farris - Circular name plate.	11 ft 9" x 6 ft (141" x 73")
John Farris - Horseshoe name plate.	11 ft 7" x 6 ft (139" x 72")
John Farris & Sons - Rectangular name plate.	12 ft x 6 ft

Height (variable) external; roof apex to ground level.

George Farris.	114"
John Farris (& Sons).	116"

Chassis construction.

Chassis: timber approx. sizes.

George Farris - Large Rectangular name plate (granary).	3" x 4" deep
George Farris - Large Rectangular name plate (s/hut).	3" x 4" deep
George Farris - Oblong name plate.	4" x 4"
George Farris - Small Oval name plate; variable.	4" x 4"
Middle chassis beams.	3" x 4" deep
John Farris - Circular name plate.	3" x 5" deep
John Farris - Horseshoe name plate.	3" x 5" deep
John Farris & Sons - Rectangular name plate.	3" x 5 deep

Number of chassis members.

George Farris huts (all).	4 main beams
	1 front
	1 rear
John Farris huts (all).	5 main beams
	1 front
	1 rear

Chassis sizes measured: in inches *(Note: variable sizes).*
George Farris - Rectangular name plate.

Granary.	Length 120 1/2" x 3" x 4" deep
	Width 72 3/8" x 3" x 4" deep

Shepherds' huts.

George Farris - Rectangular name plate.	Length 144 1/4" x 3" x 4" deep
	Width 72 3/8" x 3" x 4" deep
George Farris - Oblong name plate.	Length 144 1/4" x 4" x 4"
	Width 75 1/4" x 4" x 4"
George Farris - Small Oval name plate.	Length 143 3/4" x 4" x 4"
	Width 71 3/8" x 4" x 4"
NB. Middle beams (approx.)	143 3/4" x 3" x 4" deep
John Farris - Circular name plate.	Length 139" x 3" x 5" deep
	Width 70 1/2" x 3" x 5" deep
John Farris - Horseshoe name plate. *Variable.*	Length 137" x 3" x 5" deep
	Width 70" x 3" x 5" deep
John Farris & Sons Rectangular name plate.	*Not measured accurately*

Chassis joints.

George Farris - Stub tenon joints & mortise tenon joints.

John Farris - Mortice & tenon frame joints with wrought iron strengthening straps.

Body Construction.

Body frames.

Timber: variations in sizes in individual huts: all approx.

Three examples shown.

George Farris - Granary.

	Vertical.	3" x 3 1/8"
		2 3/4" x 3 1/4"
	Horizontal.	2" x 2 3/4" deep
	Horizontal *(below roof line).*	2 3/4" x 2 3/4"
	Additional strip between frame & roof.	1 1/2" x 1" deep

George Farris - shepherd's huts e.g. Oblong name plate.

	Vertical.	2 3/4" x 3 1/4"
	Horizontal.	2 1/2" x 2 3/4" deep
		2 3/4" x 3" deep (sides)
		2" x 3" deep (one end)
	Horizontal *(below roof line).*	3" x 3"

John Farris - Circular name plate.

	Vertical.	2 3/4" x 3"
		3" x 3"
	Horizontal.	3" x 2" deep
		3" x 1 3/4" deep
	Horizontal (below roof line).	3" x 2" deep
	Side cover board to hide gap between frame & ceiling.	1/2" x 3" deep

Corrugation:
George Farris.

Side corrugated panels width.	26"
Length approx.	72 1/2"
Roof corrugated panels.	
Length approx.	90"

John Farris.

Side corrugated panels width.	26"
Length approx.	72 1/2"
Roof corrugated panels.	
Length approx.	90"

Matchboard panelling:
Widths may be variable in similar huts.*

George Farris - Granary.	N/A
George Farris - Shepherds' huts.	
Rectangular name plate.	5 1/2"*
George Farris - Oblong.	6 1/2"
George Farris - Small Oval name plate.	5 1/2"*
John Farris - Circular name plate.	6 1/2"
John Farris - Horseshoe name plate.	6 1/2"
John Farris & Sons - Rectangular name plate.	Not measured

Windows:
These are similar for both George and John Farris huts.

Overall size approx.	21" x 14 3/4
Window glass thickness.	1/8"

Doors: *Two piece.*

Width of tongue & groove pine.	6 1/2" wide

Door frames: Width & height.

Granary (George Farris).	31" x 66"
Shepherds' huts. Approx. sizes.	31" x 68 1/2"

Interior curved central roof/ceiling supports.
Wooden.
George Farris - Rectangular name plate (granary).

	Narrow type.	2 3/8" x 2 3/8" deep

George Farris - Rectangular name plate (shepherd's hut).

	Narrow type.	2 1/4" x 2 1/4"

George Farris - Oblong name plate.	Deep type.	1 1/4" X 5 3/4 deep
George Farris - Small Oval name plate.	Deep type.	1" x 6" deep

John Farris - Circular & Horseshoe.	Wrought iron.	1 3/4" x 1/2" deep
John Farris & Sons - Rectangular.	Wooden, narrow depth.	*Not measured*

Internal ceiling heights.
(Ceiling apex to floor).

George Farris - Granary *(no panelling)*.	80 3/8"
George Farris - Shepherds' huts with panelling, approx.	80"
John Farris - Shepherds' huts with panelling, approx.	78 1/2"

Internal floor.
Variable.

George Farris - Rectangular name plate (granary).	120 1/2" x 72 3/8"

Shepherds' huts:

George Farris - Rectangular name plate.	*Not measured accurately*
George Farris - Oblong name plate.	144 5/8" x 75 1/4"
George Farris - Small Oval name plate.	143 3/4" x 71 3/8"
John Farris - Circular name plate.	139 1/4" x 70 3/4"
John Farris - Horseshoe name plate.	139" x 70 1/2
John Farris & Sons Rectangular name plate.	*Not measured accurately*

Width of floorboards.
Variable.

George Farris - Granary.	5"
George Farris - Shepherds' huts.	6 1/2"
John Farris - Shepherds' huts.	6 1/2"

Axles.
Variable sizes.

George Farris - Granary.

Wooden front top beam (3 piece).	73" x 9" x 4"
Front lower beam.	72" x 6" x 6"
Wooden rear beam.	72 x 6" x 6"

George Farris - Shepherds' huts *(various models).*
Sizes variable & approx.

Wooden front top beam.	76 3/4" x 5 3/4" x 5 3/4"
Wooden front lower beam.	76 3/4" x 5 3/4" x 5 3/4"
Wooden rear beam.	76 3/4" x 5 3/4" x 5 3/4"

John Farris - Shepherds' huts *(various models, approx. sizes).*
　　　Wooden front top beam.　　　　　　　　　70 1/2" x 6" x 6"
　　　Wooden lower beam.　　　　　　　　　　74" x 6" x 6"
　　　Front/Rear iron axles (excluding stub axles).　74" x 2" x 2"

Turntable (cast iron).
These are similar for both George and John Farris huts.
　　　Maximum width (with lugs).　　　　　　　19" (timber axle)
　　　Pin (for above).　　　　　　　　　　　18 1/2" long

Cast iron axle block castings.
For front & rear stub axles with wooden axles.

George Farris - Granary.
　　　Front.　　　　　　　　　　　　　　　6" x 2 3/4" x 3 1/4" deep
　　　Additional plate.　　　　　　　　　　6" x 2 3/4" x 7/8" thick
　　　Rear.　　　　　　　　　　　　　　　6 1/4" x 2 3/4" x 3 1/4" dee
　　　Additional plate *(including 3" lip for brace).*　9 1/4" x 2 3/4" x 7/8" thick

George Farris - Shepherds' huts.
E.g. Oblong name plate.
　　　Front.　　　　　　　　　　　　　　　6" x 2 3/4"" x 2 3/4" deep
　　　Additional plate.　　　　　　　　　　6" x 2 3/4" x 1/2" thick
　　　Rear.　　　　　　　　　　　　　　　6 x 2 3/4" x 2 3/4" deep
　　　Additional plate *(including 3" lip for brace).*　9 1/4" x 2 3/4" x 1/2" thick
　NB. Thickness of plates variable.

John Farris - Early wooden beam casting.
　　　NB. Overall depth.　　　　　　　　　6" x 2 1/2" x 5" deep

Stub axles.
Overall length. Wooden axle beams variable sizes; front & rear.

George Farris - (all).　　　　　　　　　　23 1/2"(up to approx. 25")

John Farris - (early wooden beams).　　　　28 1/2" approx.
NB: Iron axles / stub axles, one piece (front & rear).

Stub axle taper.
George Farris - Granary.　　　　　　　　　1 3/4" tapering down to 1 1/2"
George Farris - Shepherds' huts.　　　　　　*Variable*

John Farris - Shepherds' huts.　　　　　　　*Variable*

Stub axle ends.

These are similar for both George and John Farris huts.

George Farris.

Tapered length for wheel hub & cap (approx. size).

9" long

(7" to fit wheel, 2" for cap)

John Farris.

Tapered length for wheel hub & cap (approx. size).

9" long

(7" to fit wheel, 2" for cap)

Wheels.

Cast iron hub & rim, iron spokes. Variable sizes on shepherds' huts.

Early type. Front wheels: 8 spokes.

George Farris -

25" to 26"

John Farris -

25" to 26"

George Farris - Granary.

Early type. Front: 8 spokes.

26"

Shepherds' huts (see page 75).

Front wheels: 10 spokes.

George Farris -

24 1/2"

John Farris -

24 1/2"

Rear wheels: All

10 spokes. Approx. sizes.

George Farris -

3 ft

John Farris -

3 ft

Hub caps.

x 4

Horse shafts.

Eg. Ash. George and John Farris huts.

Hardwood

Stove.

E.g. Portman tortoise No 2.

Optional (23" high x 12" wide).

Flue.

3"

Flue casting: max. width (ribbed for roof sheets).

George Farris -

8 1/4" x 7 1/2"

John Farris -

8 1/4" x 7 1/2"

Flue cap.

George Farris -

Yes

John Farris -

Yes

Variable = slight variations in size.

Brief measurement guide: 1" = approx. 25mm. 12" = 1ft = approx. 30cm.

Collectable farming bygones

This book has been predominately about Sybil and the history of her grandfather, George Farris, at the Coombe Bissett Steam Plough works, and the remarkable shepherds' huts and granaries that they produced.

The following information is a brief description of some of the many interesting 19th and early 20th century shepherd, sheep and unusual agricultural related items that can be used to help decorate ones own historic hut, or even bought as collectible items to display in their own

1929 Bibby's feed advert.

right. Many of these items are becoming increasingly difficult to find and may need some sympathetic restoration carried out on them due to their age, hard use and neglect. Discovering rare and unusual pieces can be rewarding and exciting, and often very educational, although finding them at affordable prices and in reasonable condition due to their rarity and antiquity is becoming more challenging.

The most obvious items for displaying in a shepherd's hut are crooks, sheep bells (e.g. canister, clucket and rumbler bells) and lanterns.

Antique shepherds crooks with a forged iron head and a wooden ash or hazel shaft are particularly sought after and come in a variety of shapes and sizes. Be aware of examples with names or numbers on as these are likely to have been adapted from an old tool, such as a hoe. The quality, condition and prices of crooks can also vary considerably.

Some of the better examples were made from gun barrels, normally distinguishable with a furrow running around the outside of its loop (but easily confused with a groove or furrow made by a good blacksmith that was included for strength), a narrow shank, and usually with a perfect large open whorl (about 1 1/4" diameter) on the end.

Sheep crooks made in the Downland's during the 19th century are reputed to be some of the best ever made, with Berry of Pyecombe being the best known, but Hoather of Kingston- by- Lewes, and Green of Falmer, also producing excellent examples in their day, with perfect large whorls. Often crooks are called 'Pyecombe' but are not always the genuine thing!

Crooks were usually designed to catch a sheep by its hind leg although it's also possible to discover antique examples that were made to catch sheep (or lambs) by the neck. These crooks subsequently had a wider mouth (and loop) and are known as neck crooks. The heavy Romney March Looker's Crook is an exceptionally good example of this type of design.

Sometimes, what at first appears to be a shepherds crook is actually a tool that was used in apple orchards for pulling branches towards the picker for harvesting purposes. Shepherds leg crooks curve slightly backwards at the tapered socket end before curving forward to form the loop of the crook, usually being finished with a single or double whorl or peened over rounded end. It's certainly worth studying examples of crooks in detail before making a purchase as there are some reproductions appearing for sale that look old, so be cautious!

A poultry geese crook is another variant that looks like a shepherds crook but is generally smaller in size and has a narrower (approx. 5/8") gap across the mouth. Larger shepherds leg crooks are commonly between 1" and 1 1/4" across, although it is possible to discover original examples with slightly wider gaps. There's a tendency for some shepherds crooks to be called geese crooks, with an inflated price tag attached to them!

Dipping crooks, used for dipping sheep, are interesting and rare additions to a crook collection and are usually distinguishable by two iron loops (on the end of a long wooden shaft) facing opposite directions, but designs can vary. One loop was used for pushing the sheep under the water, the other loop for pulling the sheep upwards. Early dipping crooks made completely from wood (e.g. elm and ash) are also highly collectable but are becoming hard to find in reasonable condition.

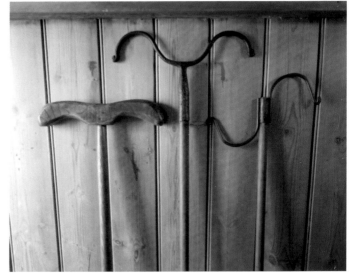

Sheep bells seem to come in all shapes and sizes with some of the most desirable being canister, clucket, crotal, latten and cup bells, and were popular with shepherds during the 18th and 19th centuries. They certainly had a practical use as they provided a shepherd with an awareness of where his sheep were. If the bells started to produce an erratic sound rather than a gentle clunk or ring, there was a good chance that the sheep were running, thereby warning the shepherd that they might be in danger.

Canister and clucket bells were normally hand made by the local blacksmith from sheet metal and riveted, usually had an iron clapper, and can show remnants of brass on them that originates from their manufacture. Some early examples have a metal 'm' shaped fitting on top to allow the bell to be held by a leather strap.

Other bells collected by shepherds were cast by bell-founders, but were generally more expensive. These were crotal bells (rumblers), sphere in shape that has a tiny metal ball inside to make a sound, latten bells (classic bell shape) and cup bells (shape of an upturned cup), with both latter examples having a metal clapper.

Wooden bell yokes, often made from yew and carefully carved by the shepherd, are sometimes discovered with their initials or markings on and were used to attach bells such as canister and clucket bells around the sheep's neck. Leather straps were placed through the bell and yoke then secured with two hand made yew or bone lockyers (e.g. pegs). Leather yokes and collars were also commonly used. Old wooden yokes have a lovely smooth and worn feel to them.

Tin candle lanterns are another excellent item to include in a shepherd's hut. Early 18th century examples can on occasion be found with their original horn windows although expect some damage to them due to their age. Lanterns were cylindrically shaped with a conical top that included holes or 'dormer' vents and had a very simple candle holder positioned centrally inside the base. A small opening

door was included in order to easily light and extinguish the candle flame. A soft sulphur yellow glow through the horn was produced by these lanterns and was well favoured by shepherds. English horn lanterns are extremely sought after by collectors and the price they achieve at auction reflects this. Certain styles would have been more suitable for shepherds which comprised of smaller windows with a thin wire guard in front of the horn to offer additional protection. Some horn lanterns are quite large and have huge windows with horn (without protective wire guards) and were generally more suited to taverns or street lighting. Early examples of lanterns made with translucent sheets of horn were known as lanthorns.

Cylindrically shaped lanterns were gradually redesigned to incorporate cheaper flat panes of glass, and rectangular lanterns with glass windows also became popular. During the later part of the 19th century the availability of curved glass allowed for an array of designs to be made. More modern candle lanterns with glass are probably the more practical option for the 21st century, although the occasional use of an antique horn lantern flickering in a shepherd's hut feels magical.

Docking irons (for sheep tails), braziers (to heat docking irons), marking irons and ruddle pot (used for sheep marking), sheep shears and wooden yolks, drenching horns and feeding bottles are all sheep related items that display well in a hut. Old iron chains hung from hooks also give a rustic agricultural charm, as do old leather straps and harnesses, although too many chains and leather could give a wrong impression!

Agricultural smocks (traditionally worn by rural workers such as shepherds and agricultural labourers), wooden oak drinking costrel (for the shepherds beverage), fold pitching iron (used for hurdles), hay fork, turnip pick and hand turnip chopper (used for winter feeding), stool, trunk, thatching needle, salve pot (for sheep ointment), Manchur's balance (for weighing wool), sheep dipping advertising signs and tins (e.g. Coopers, Mc Dougall's & Robertson), cooking utensils and kettle, the list could go on.

One intriguing piece of furniture that I have seen displayed in a hut was a 'lambing chair'. They were reputedly originally used by shepherds around the late 18th to early 19th centuries during lambing time in the northern regions of England, notably in Lancashire & Yorkshire. Construction was of wood (e.g. pine, elm, oak), with tall back and 'winged arms', and often consisted of a storage facility under the seat. Smaller rustic versions look very in keeping in a shepherd's house, adding an early period feature with character.

Some collections can become quite extensive over the years, and in this instance it is advisable to consider the security aspect of displaying too many of them in your hut at one time, especially the rarer and more expensive items. Unless you have a vicious looking dog patrolling your pride and joy night and day, it's probably prudent to keep the more valuable items in a safer place and display them in your hut when you are using it, rather than on a permanent basis.

Granaries may be a little more difficult to decorate with a period agricultural theme. A tin candle lantern, agricultural smock, an early traditional seed-lip (used to hold seed whilst hand broadcasting), iron chains, wooden casting shovel (used when winnowing or 'dressing' the corn), fine meshed sieve, large hand carved birch wood grain scoop, wooden measuring grain bucket (or bushel), broom, old stool (or chair), large vintage hessian sacks (to store grain in), antique grain sampling probe (for checking the quality of the harvest during storage) and a traditional forged hook to

help lift the sacks (when carrying on ones back), would all help to create an authentic setting.

Vintage grain sacks are increasingly becoming harder to discover in reasonable condition and are very large (50" x 25" approx.) and heavy duty. They may include a company name, location and even a date printed on them.

Traditional harvesting tools such as a hand scythe or sickle could also be used in a display. Good examples are still fairly easy to find so it's worth being selective and purchasing decent ones.

A rare 19th century English corn hand flail (also referred to as a 'stick and a half'), was used for threshing to separate grain from their husks, and would certainly be a notable addition. Flails normally have a long thin tapered wooden staff (e.g.

Arable farm tools.

approx. 4 1/2 ft long), which was held by the farm labourer, and were often turned from hardwoods, such as ash or beech, usually with a blacksmith forged 'eye' on the end or stitched leather sleeve and socket. An alternative method used was for a matching piece of hardwood to be skilfully shaped and curved to form an eye, then attached to the staff end. A similar style of eye but with a wooden swivel head (or hood) was also a good design and can be found on some American flails.

The beater (or swipple) which struck the grain was shorter (e.g. approx. 2ft long) and might be made with the same type of hardwood, or possibly from a suitable piece of gnarled wood from the hedgerow, such as holly. The ends commonly had a bound leather sleeve and socket. Both staff and swipple on English flails are usually attached loosely together with a leather thong or sometimes a short forged chain incorporating a swivel fitting.

The craftsmanship of flails can vary enormously, with some examples looking very rustic (with bark still attached) and perhaps a little crude in their appearance, whilst others have been carefully made to form very attractive tools.

Flails often show signs of a hard life, but their rarity definitely makes them worth adding to an agricultural theme if lucky enough to discover one. Apart from the odd worm holes or splits in the wooden staff and beater to contend with, the aged leather

174

parts of flails are inevitably cracked and brittle, but can usually be repaired and preserved and made more supple by carefully applying a good quality hide cream.

Corn was traditionally harvested in the summer and was either bound into sheafs, or taken loose by cart, to be stored in a barn ready for threshing in the autumn. Threshing would have been carried out with wooden hand flails before the winnowing process began in preparation for the grain to be sent to the mill. Even with the introduction of threshing machines, powered by steam, they were still used by some smaller farms during the early 20th century.

Along with antique shepherds crooks, flails are one of my favourite hand tools, each one being individually made, thereby assuring subtle differences in design and character. Many crooks were regularly used and carefully looked after by shepherds, who repaired or replaced broken wooden shafts when necessary. Flails however, generally took a pounding during the threshing process by farm labourers doing a very laborious and exhausting task, and didn't always receive the care and attention that they deserved, thus making good original examples exceedingly difficult to find.

A 'bere' or barley hummeller (an early blacksmith made forged hand tool, either square, round or rectangular in design and usually with a wooden 'T' shaped shaft) was used to remove the beards (or awns) of barley after threshing. Once common in the south west of England (e.g. West Country), they are now increasingly difficult to find but would also make an excellent addition to a farming collection. A period advert in a 1879 edition of 'The Engineer' describes them as a barley horner.

Continuing to stretch the imagination a little more with curious barley related hand tools (c.1900), a barley stooking (or sheaf) fork that was used to move large sheaves of barley, is another harvesting rarity. The more substantial examples, measuring in the region of 5ft long by 19" wide overall, can appear quite sculptural with their huge curved wrought iron prongs and wooden 'T' handle. Slightly smaller sized sheaf forks would perhaps be more suitable for displaying in a granary. Apparently they were very popular in areas such as East Anglia and the West Country and have become increasingly scarce to find in more recent years. As barley is also an important ingredient of beer, these impressive early tools associated with this versatile arable crop will appeal to collectors of both farming and brewery antiques.

Agricultural corn dibber's (or setting irons) are collectable items. Consisting of a wooden shaft with an iron shank with bulbous pointed end, or sometimes forged almost completely in wrought iron with a wooden hand grip (sizes vary, but usually about 3ft long), they were originally used to aid the sowing of corn before more efficient seed drills became available during the 19th century. If fortunate enough to own one, they can be a very useful and practical tool around a productive garden or allotment.

An uncommon find would be an early 19th century pitch pine 'hicking stick'. This was a simple form of hand barrow, thought to originate from the Middle Ages, and was used to aid the loading of large hessian sacks of grain into a cart. Hand made by country craftsmen, these carved strong sticks were usually about 38" long, with approximately 1 5/8" square middle section, tapering down to around 1 1/4" rounded ends that were comfortable to hold when lifting. Some examples were designed with a thicker 'stepped down' square middle section. The stick was placed under the sack of grain and lifted by two labourers, one either side of it. If the sack was not evenly placed in the middle of the stick when carrying it the heavy weight would be distributed unevenly. I believe this may be where the phrase 'got the short end of the stick' originated from. The short end was the heaviest!

I have also seen a similar shaped stick adapted into a 19th century log puller. Constructed of a straight piece of oak measuring 48" long, with square middle section and round tapered ends, two blacksmith made curved hooks were held together by a rivet and centrally positioned and attached by three links of chain secured by a bolt through the stick. These hooks would be tightened and clasp onto the log as it was dragged along. Other log pullers that I have seen are usually more rustic in appearance with signs of hard use, having a simple round middle section and tapered ends with a blacksmith sleeve made to fit centrally along the shaft, and curved hooks attached accordingly.

Another useful item used for carrying purposes was the timber hand barrow, without a wheel. Smaller sizes tend to be about 44" x 16" overall and required one person either end to carry it. They were of a simple design but usually beautifully made from a hardwood timber such as elm. Two main beams were shaped and curved upwards at the ends to form handles, with three cross spars, that were mortised, pinned and chamfered to create a strong 'rack' construction. They were ideal for carrying sheaves of corn and sacks of goods on the farm. Smaller barrows were also useful as a millers sack carrier. Larger and more heavy duty examples with additional cross spars were handy for moving rocks and heavier goods over rough ground. It is still possible to discover 19th century wooden hand barrows in reasonable condition, although there's a tendency for the handle ends to show signs of deterioration if the rack has been left standing on its end in a damp barn for a long time.

Other agricultural related items such as a vintage sack lifting truck (to aid the lifting of sacks of grain into a cart or granary) and some sack weighing scales, would certainly raise serious doubts to ones sanity, but once hooked by this hobby, anything goes!

Hurdles look undeniably impressive associated with shepherds' houses and granaries and can be used outside to create a traditional setting. One doesn't have to build a sheep fold though, as a few hurdles (e.g. hazel or willow) positioned to keep the prevailing wind at bay, and possibly to enclose a small and intimate seating area, is always a pleasurable experience.

Larger agricultural implements such as a vintage cast iron root chopper (used to chop turnips and mangolds for sheep) or an early shearing machine would also provide additional interest, and relate to a traditional shepherd and lambing theme.

Now, If you happen to own a collie and a few sheep!!

HAYWARD'S SHEEP DIPS

Approved by the Board of Agriculture, and used in all Sheep Countries.

HAYWARD'S

Yellow Paste Dip.
Combined Glycerine Dip.
Liquid Dips.
Non-Poisonous Paste
    and Cake Dips.

Attractively packed with Agent's own
name if desired.

HAYWARD'S

Foot Rot Paste and Liquid.
Sheep Marking Paints.
Lung Worm Specific.
Warble Fly Smear.
Luddington's Oils.
Condition Powders, and
Veterinary Medicines.

GOOD SELLERS!   GOOD PROFITS!   ATTRACTIVE ADVERTISING MATTER!

Write for Particulars
to Sole Manufacturers   **TOMLINSON & HAYWARD, Ltd., LINCOLN.**

WALKER, TROKE & CO.
WHOLESALE DRUGGISTS,
(late 65) Bath St., City Road,
LONDON, E.C.
Telephone: "3593 CENTRAL."

GELATINE-COATED DOG & FOWL
PILLS.   Samples Free.
Sole Makers of 'SANOGEN VAPORISER' (Reg. No. 21.772), for **WHOOPING COUGH, ASTHMA, &c.** Retail Price 2/6 (subj. to dis.

SOLE MAKERS OF
GABRIEL & TROKE'S
GELATINE CAPSULED
HORSE BALLS

Alterative, Condition, Cordial, Cough
Diuretic,   Fever,   Physic,   Worm
Quinine, Tonic Balls (Registered 81,291)

IT PAYS YOU TO STOCK

DENNIS'S

"LINCOLNSHIRE"

PIG POWDERS,

THEY YIELD A GOOD PROFIT.
HAVE THE LARGEST SALE.

DENNIS'S LINCOLNSHIRE PIG POWDERS
PROPRIETOR J.W. DENNIS
LOUTH.
ENGLAND

Registered Trade Mark No. 14,839.

IT WILL PAY EQUALLY WELL TO STOCK

DENNIS'S SPECIAL

WORM POWDERS FOR PIGS.

Sold in 6d. and 1/- Packets.

"CARROTINE," THE BEST and STRONGEST,

Purely VEGETABLE BUTTER COLOURING.

Wholesale Agents : ALL PATENT MEDICINE DEALERS.
Wholesale Prices. Handbills with name at foot, Show Cards, &c.,
from the Proprietor—

J. W. DENNIS, Chemist, LOUTH.

CARROTINE.
Trade Mark No. 27,972.

Advertisements c.1911 promoting sheep & other animal health products.

An inspirational way of displaying plants.

The quality, simplicity and even ingenuity of some early farming hand tools make interesting and unusual additions to a collection when able to locate and purchase them, and subsequently provides enthusiasts with a broad and fascinating area to explore.

The diversity of farming can lead the enthusiast down many paths, including land drainage tools (e.g. specialised spades, forks, picks), cultivating implements (e.g. ploughs, harrows, hoes), farm dairy tools and equipment (e.g. curd breakers, milking stools), as well as general land maintenance tools for hedge laying, etc.

Whether a serious collector or interested purely for nostalgic and historic reasons, collection and preservation of earlier and unusual antique tools is immensely enjoyable, and sympathetic restoration of them is always desirable. Some farm tools are becoming so rare that they are destined to only be admired in museums dedicated to rural life.

Later vintage hand tools and implements from around the 1920's onwards, including both farming and horticultural examples, are still reasonably affordable and are taking on a new lease of life. Many are being restored to use in gardens and allotments. Although some were mass produced, the quality, feel and therapeutic attributes sets them apart from their modern equivalents, and continues the acknowledgement and interest that these old practical tools and implements have earned.

Types of wood

The following list of trees and shrubs are examples of woods previously mentioned and commonly used by shepherds and country craftsmen when making their hand tools and equipment. The original wood of old hand tools usually have an aged richness of colour and patina specific to the type of wood used, and when cleaned and preserved with bees wax can make remarkably attractive displays. All Genus are hardwoods unless otherwise specified.

Latin name	Common name
Betula pendula	Birch
Corylus avellana	Hazel
Cratageous monogyna	Hawthorn *
Fagus sylvatica	Beech
Fraxinus species	Ash
Ilex aquifolium	Holly
Pinus species	Pine (softwood)
Prunus spinosa	Blackthorn *
Quercus robur	Oak
Salix species	Willow
Taxus baccata	Yew (hard softwood)
Ulmus species	Elm

* included as useful hedgerow hardwoods

Many of the attractive woods below are generally more common in professions such as cabinet and musical instrument making. However, they can on the odd occasion be found used on quality 19th century hand tools and equipment, including fine equine and veterinary items.

Latin name	Common name
Acer pseudoplatanus	Sycamore
Alnus glutinosa	Alder
Buxus sempervirens	Boxwood
Carya species	Hickory
Cedrus species	Cedar (softwood)
Dalbergia species	Rosewood
Diospyros species	Ebony
Guaiacum species	Lignum vitae
Juglans regia	Walnut
Malus, Prunus & Pyrus species, etc.	Fruitwood
Swietenia species	Mahogany
Tectona gandis	Teak
Tilia species	Lime

Model shepherds' huts

For people who do not have the facilities, time or resources for restoring a full size shepherd's hut (or granary) building models could be an enjoyable alternative. It is possible to find miniature shepherds' huts in white metal, 1:43 kit form (0 scale), with accessories such as a stove and flue.

Improvements can be made by making a wooden floor and interior side panels from very thin plywood which is commonly used in model making. The addition of thin ply is also useful as it can be carefully steamed to the curved shape of the roof (and ceiling) enabling the roof sheets to be easily attached to it. Reducing the length of a model shepherd's hut and omitting a window, stove and flue, provides the basis for a granary.

Including model sheep, a dog, shepherd and perhaps a hurdle or two with a few miniature plants, can make a very authentic display, especially if painted impressionistically. You never know, in some very small way it might even stimulate ones interest to become an historic hut enthusiast, and that has to be a positive outcome!

Vintage farming machinery and implements such as steam engines, threshing machines, straw elevators, horse drawn carts and ploughs, plus farm animals and labourers, are all available in metal kit form from model specialists, thereby enabling different themes to be created and allowing the model enthusiast endless ways to absorb themselves in this delicate and intriguing hobby.

Small vintage lead farming or shepherd figures, animals, hurdles, fencing, gates, and foliage, may also be interesting subjects to include in a display if found to be of a suitable size and in reasonable condition, and are becoming increasingly sought after by model collectors. Lead models obviously have some health and safety concerns, but their rarity does make them fascinating additions to a collection and adds some vintage nostalgia.

Steam Fairs

Enthusiasts of original shepherds' houses often enjoy steam fairs and subsequently display their huts at this type of rally. The restorations are usually sympathetic and of a very good standard.

The Great Dorset Steam Fair is a particular favourite (and the best) as it usually attracts around at least twenty five historic huts, such as Farris, Lott & Walne, Reeves, and Watson & Haig. Living vans are also popular and can be found mingling among the steam traction engines.

Exhibitors are extremely friendly and helpful and make fellow enthusiasts feel very welcome indeed. To see historic shepherds' huts being used and enjoyed by their owners and families is always a pleasant experience, and is one of the most important aspects of this hobby, regardless of the originality or condition of a hut that one owns.

Although original detailing is an important consideration of a shepherds' huts preservation, ones personal feelings towards a specific hut can often outweigh many other factors. A memory, a notable occasion, or the overall atmosphere and historic character of a hut shines through and makes it special. Imperfections and originality become secondary, as overall attraction dominates ones emotions and thoughts.

John Farris's great grandson has a fascinating stand at The Great Dorset Steam Fair and displays his grandfathers (Charles Farris) superb miniature steam engine and wonderful collection of John Farris (& Sons) memorabilia.

Enthusiasts show a tremendous commitment when displaying at shows, as apart from the time and preparation it takes to display their huts, the transportation can be quite difficult and expensive. Some local shepherds' huts owners use large trailers, but a low loader lorry is usually more appropriate for longer distances. Shows are also good places to look at other agricultural exhibits, and a valuable place to make new contacts and friends and find missing parts for a restoration project that may be in progress. Exhibiting at steam fairs may not interest, or be suitable for some people, but it's certainly an enjoyable day out and helps contribute towards the valuable preservation of these wonderful shepherds' houses.

Personally, I have not indulged myself with the delights of the rally scene yet, but tend to appreciate the simplicity of preserving and displaying shepherds' houses either in my garden or small wildflower meadow. A place to step back in time, socialise with family and friends, or inspire me whilst writing this book. Shepherds' houses (and granaries) can be addictive, seductive, and in some cases, awe inspiring due to their history. For years many have been ravaged by time, weather and neglect. Today, they are being lovingly restored and gaining the appreciation they deserve as antiquities in their own right. Surely a fitting tribute to the hard working men who built them all those years ago!

Postscript:

Sybil moved from her grandfathers old cottage at Bissett Coombe in July 2012, as she said it was becoming too difficult to keep on top of the garden, field, ponies and chickens, where the foundry was originally located. At the age of 95, I was not surprised! She sold it to a distant relative of Charles Farris (who died from a riding accident in 1879), thereby continuing the occupancy of the Farris family at the cottages.

At the time of publishing my book, Sybil is 97 years of age. She is surely the oldest hut enthusiast that I have had the privilege to know and will certainly be the most inspirational!

Farris shepherd's hut register

This is a register for all Farris shepherd's hut owners and enthusiasts whose huts have been made at either the Coombe Bissett or Shaftesbury Works. The register is intended purely as a guide for the number of George Farris and John Farris huts which may have survived over the years. Condition is not important. Sybil and her family will be kept updated on the numbers of huts known to exist.

Name.
Contact details.

Hut Details.
George Farris.
John Farris.
Shepherd's hut or granary?
Maker or type of hut unknown.

Points of interest.
E.g. Name plate included?
    Size of hut.
    Type of axles.
    Condition.

Photographs.
    Exterior.
    Interior.

Additional information.

Please contact:

Rollin Nicholls at rollinspublications@gmail.com.

All enquiries will be acknowledged.

Thank you.

New Discoveries

(Quick Check List)

Example.

Contact details.	Unknown
Address.	Coombe Bissett
Tel. No.	Unknown

Make of hut.	Farris ... name plate attached
Type of hut.	Granary
Age.	Victorian/Edwardian
Body size.	10ft x 6ft approx.
Condition.	Good. One roof sheeting with hole & some ragged edges
Body frame	
Condition.	Very sound overall
Chassis	
Condition	Signs of rot in rear beam (near side). Overall good
Axle type.	Wooden axles
Condition.	Damage to front axle ends. Rear axle good ... a few cracks in the wood
Wheel type/size.	Original Farris wheels with spokes
	Wheel sizes 2ft & 3ft approx.
Condition.	Very good but slight buckle to one of the rear wheels
Internal panelling.	
Condition.	N/a as granary
Window.	
Condition.	N/a as granary
Door.	
Condition.	Good ... not original ... stable type
Steps.	
Condition.	Need replacing ... Original brackets present
Floor type.	Softwood ... pine
Condition.	Very good overall ... a few rear boards may need replacing
Stove/flue.	
Condition.	N/a as granary

184

Horse shafts/tow bar.

Condition.   Iron tow bar present. No wooden shafts.

Points of interest.   Owned by Sybil, the granddaughter of George Farris
                              An early granary .... not a shepherd's hut
                              Original corrugated panels
                              Original wheels fitted
                              Horse shaft hook fitted
                              Interesting writing on the interior frame and corrugated
                              sheets, including a date

Location of hut.   Near main road ... A354 Coombe Bissett
                              Narrow drive ... Soft ground
                              Ponies in paddock
                              Wheels have seized & leaning against hut
                              Some damage to rear axle bolts
                              Signs of someone living in the hut

Additional notes.   Will require a lorry with crane due to seized wheels
                              and soft ground

R. & J. REEVES & SON'S CATALOGUE.

REEVES' IMPROVED SHEPHERD'S HUT, OR PORTABLE GRANARY.

Inspiration

Meeting Sybil has been a great privilege. Her generosity in allowing me to purchase her treasured portable granary and providing details of her ancestral family history, with kind permission to include in my book, has given me the inspiration to write an accurate, in depth, historical account, not just on Farris huts, but also on Sybil's grandfather, George Farris, of the Bissett Coombe Steam Plough Works, near Salisbury.

I have enjoyed some very special moments listening to Sybil's fascinating stories about her grandfather and family. Her attention to detail has been meticulous and authoritative, her sense of humour a pleasure. A chance comment resulting in the discovery of a historic granary, and a friendship with the extraordinary granddaughter of George Farris has been a wonderful experience.

Comparing details of Sybil's granary with other shepherds' huts, made by both George and his brother, John, has allowed for some interesting comparisons to be made and discussed during my on going research, and acts as a useful and authoritative guide for both the Farris enthusiast and collector. Hopefully, this will encourage and help new and existing owners contemplating restoring original examples made either by Farris, or by one of their competitors, to sympathetically renovate them back as close to their original condition as possible. Not only will this contribute to preserving part of our rural heritage for future generations to enjoy, but will also provide accurate historical evidence of the different types of huts built during the late 19th and early 20th centuries.

The following poems
are dedicated to my best friend

True Love

Lying in the tall meadow grasses,
Relaxing within my inner soul,
A beauty resting beside me,
Her breast moving with every breath.

Contemplating her gentle movements,
Fingers touch, with tingling response,
Powerful feelings of affection,
Lightning explodes all around!

Birds singing with all their joy
Drowning the sound of her soft voice,
Aromas stimulating the senses
As our hearts become one.

Emotions of childhood sweethearts,
Lovers and best friends for life,
Dreams seem to go on forever,
Memories and thoughts linger on.

Happiness from our offspring,
Cheerfulness in our minds,
Wonders of what the future holds,
Vivid images of the past.

A smile that drifts in the wind,
Eyes sparkling with delight,
Laughter to brighten each day,
A true love that will last forever!

Rollin

188

Floating on the breeze

A simple glance across the room,
Dislocated thoughts, to confuse the mind.
Feeling the heat from her piercing eyes
With a smile so alluring to tantalise the heart.

Moments of affection, forever at the fore,
Fragments of memories fusing as one,
Two soft voices whispering in harmony
As inquisitiveness and laughter prevails.

Passion lingers with every conversation,
Bodies clinging without a fight,
Chemistry bonding lovers together
Peacefully entwined in each others arms.

Expressions of happiness appearing on the face,
Fingers following the curve of the spine,
Eyelids close with gentle persuasion
As the tenderness of love floats on the breeze.

Rollin

Reflections

Chasing reflections of a distant memory,
Sounds of happiness drifting through the night,
Warmth of bodies drawing closer together,
Softness of her lips, in the dappled light,

Lingering fragrance stimulating the senses,
Wondrous feelings pounding at the heart,
Blown away on a whirlwind of emotion,
Tenderness of lovers that will never part.

Unspoken words till the twilight hours,
Catching some rays from the morning sun,
Gradually melting from the heat of the moment,
Bodies and minds, forever as one!

Rollin

Buttercup Meadow by Rollin

Acknowledgements

All research for my book has been independently carried out by myself. The following acknowledgements are dedicated to family, friends and enthusiasts who have whole-heartedly helped me achieve my goal.

Thank you.

I wish to thank Sybil Spinks, granddaughter of George Farris, and her daughter Angela for their enthusiasm and support whilst writing this book, and for being so helpful and generous with providing some unique historical information and pictures about their family ancestor, George Farris of the Coombe Bissett Steam Plough Works.

I am also grateful to fellow hut enthusiast, craftsman and friend, Eddie Butterfield of Butterfield Ironworks, Shitterton, Dorset, whose extensive knowledge and advice on restorations and building traditional shepherds' huts has been invaluable. With over twenty years experience of restoring shepherds' huts, including many Farris examples, I am indebted to him for his time, energy and patience in helping me clarify some of the technical details and information during my research on Farris shepherds' huts. Thank you!

My appreciation and thanks goes to fellow enthusiasts whose huts I have been allowed to photograph and study, and for their kindness in taking the time to confirm a few details about them. A special mention also to Cotswold Shepherds' Huts and Sunny Meadows Shepherds' Huts.

Thank you to Ray Farris for his interesting conversations and comments about his great grandfather's Shaftesbury business and shepherds' huts.

My thanks to Tony Munt and Sue Wiles for generously providing their beautiful horse Achellia, during a special evening arranged for Sybil.

I wish to acknowledge Julien of julien@media4.co.uk for the professional preparation and advice on the design and layout of my book. Thank you.

A special thank you to members of my family and friends, for your continued support, and for also giving me the confidence to include a few of my poems and paintings.

Last but not least, a huge thank you to my incredibly tolerant wife and best friend, and our wonderful children, for continuing to put up with my eccentricities and allowing me the freedom to realise a dream!

NB All measurements are in imperial (and approx.) to co-ordinate with a Farris huts original manufacture.

Disclaimer: *The author accepts no liability for technical or practical information provided in this book, and readers should seek professional help and advice as required.*